THE 4 SECRETS TO COLLEGE *life* SUCCESS

*How to thrive in your life
during and after college*

CLINT PARDOE

The 4 Secrets To College Life Success

How to thrive in your life during and after college

ISBN: 978-1-61170-003-9

Printed in the United States of America on acid-free paper.

Cover design by Christopher Otazo

Photo by Tanja Lippert

"Life" logo by Paul Salamone

 **Robertson Publishing**
59 N. Santa Cruz Avenue, Suite B
Los Gatos, California 95030 USA
888) 354-5957 • www.RobertsonPublishing.com

To my wife Jennifer, my daughter Coral, and my son Curren—
My life is a success largely due to you.

Contents

INTRODUCTION

Hawaii. Unlike most of my high school friends, I chose not to go to Mexico for my senior graduation trip. Instead, my two best friends joined me and another friend of ours for a month long vacation in Hawaii. Yes, one month; of surfing, drinking and, despite my insecurities, picking up on girls. Good thing we had John with us. John would pick up on anyone. Girls either loved him or they hated him. And, despite the numerous girls that were appalled by his behavior, there were a few who weren't… and this was good news for the rest of us. One such girl was Katie. And, although her friends were pretty "hot," she was the envy of everyone in our group. And, guess who she ended up spending the entire vacation with? John.

California. Shortly after returning from Hawaii, my friends and I continued our celebration back home in California. Still living at my parents' house, I had managed to figure out a way not to work that summer; so I continued to spend most of my time surfing, drinking and picking up on girls. One of our favorite places to go out every week was at a local club that held "youth nights," where it was open to ages sixteen years old and over. One of these nights, as I was probably doing my "I look confident but I'm really masking my low self-esteem" dance amidst a crowd of people, I was surprisingly approached by a girl that looked very similar to John's Katie in Hawaii. As her and I began dancing with each other, she quickly reminded me about a party earlier that year where I had met her and her friends. While I remembered the party and her friends, to be honest, I didn't remember her; and at that point, it didn't matter.

We ended up dancing with each other that night until the club closed and then, surprisingly, she proceeded to ask me out. However, with the question came the story. This girl, Leanne, had just ended a two year relationship because she wanted to be "free" to date different people her senior year of high school. I was cool with that…for a while.

Serious. Prior to meeting Leanne, I had never been in a serious relationship and it wasn't until I met her that I felt ready. So, despite her not wanting to be in one, I was determined to change her plans. After spending the rest of the summer together, school finally began; she was a senior in high school and I was a freshman in college. It was only a few weeks into the school year when I found out that Leanne, despite her heart wanting to be in a relationship with me, followed her head and accepted being asked to her first formal dance by another guy. Rather than express my feelings about the situation, I did the only thing I knew how to do during that time; I got pissed and cut things off.

Once Leanne realized that I was serious about not seeing her anymore, I received a lengthy letter from her that expressed how she had made a mistake and how she was willing to be in a committed relationship with me; even if I chose to date other people. I chose to date other people, alright…and Leanne wasn't one of them.

Safety. For the next few years, I dated many different girls and *knew* that, no matter what, Leanne would always be there to take me back…even if I was eventually divorced with fifteen children. Almost every time I would stop dating someone, she was the first person I would contact and briefly hang out with; I always wanted to make sure the safety net was still in place.

Best friend. As I was about to graduate from college, I was living with my best friend, Raoul. I've known Raoul since I can remember, and he's been more like a brother to me than a best friend. And, because of this, he was there when I would talk crap about Leanne, glare at her at parties, and I think he even witnessed the day I spit on her car. If anyone knew how angry I was at her over the years, it was him. But what he didn't know, what nobody knew, was that all of my anger was masking deep hurt; hurt that only comes from caring. So, when Leanne showed up at our house one evening after going to the movies with Raoul, I became extremely jealous. I couldn't lie to myself or anyone else any longer. To Raoul's surprise, I proceeded to share my feelings about Leanne with him and, like a good best friend would, he immediately backed off any potential relationship pursuit. Admitting this was a relief, but it also reignited my feelings for her; which became complicated, being as I was in the midst of my first-ever long-term romantic relationship.

Break-up. My newly unburied feelings for Leanne were essentially what prompted me to end this relationship. Not only did I tip-toe around the break up by eventually telling my girlfriend of a year and a half that "I would call her back if I changed my mind," but, due to my insecurities, I also took a long time to break it off; which, by the time that I did, Leanne had moved on to another guy.

Unknown. Have you ever thought that, with every cell in your body, you absolutely knew something to be true and, come to find out, it was completely different than what you thought? Remember when I mentioned earlier that I *knew* Leanne would always be there for me, ready to take me back at the drop of a hat? Well, that ended up not being the case. Even though I lagged on breaking up with my ex-girlfriend and Leanne was in a new relationship, I thought she would drop everything to be with me once I was single; and she didn't. This threw me into the unknown; and with this uncertainty, came severe anxiety.

Public Speaking. Prior to this, the only time I remember being really anxious was when I was required to give a speech and, funny enough, one of my favorite classes in college was public speaking. During this time of uncertainty, my younger sister was taking public speaking from the same instructor that I had taken it with. I don't remember exactly why, but I asked my sister to ask my former instructor if I could visit the class one day; which he was more than happy to let me do. That day changed the direction of my life.

During that class, the instructor mentioned the benefits of becoming a speech teacher at the college level and, being as I was about to graduate from college with a degree that I had no idea what I was going to do with, I decided that I wanted to do that. However, after speaking with him about this, the first step in the process required I do something that I never thought I would do; go to graduate school.

Master. After graduation, I had about nine months before I could go back to school to purse my Masters Degree in Communication Studies, so I ended up taking another graduation trip back to Hawaii with a similar group of friends, as well a solo trip to Europe. As time went on, my anxiety worsened and eventually led into depression, and my depression led me to the self-help section at bookstores. My friends would invite me out to do the same thing we had been doing for years (drinking and picking up on girls) and I would choose to go to a bookstore and read. In addition to mastering communication, through books, I was intent upon life mastery as well.

Love. After reading more books in nine months than I had throughout my entire life, I came across *Gifts from the Heart: 10 ways to build more loving relationships* by Randy Fujishin, and my main goal, different from the angry person I had become, was to be a more loving human being to others.

One way I did this was by signing up to run a marathon (26.2 miles) through *Team in Training*, a program created by the Leukemia Society to support people's athletic goals while raising money for Leukemia research. However, after running crazy long miles every week in preparation for the event, I began to experience severe back pain. After sharing this with my yoga instructor at the time, he recommended a great chiropractor.

Jennifer. After some deep introspection in the area of romantic relationships, I was pretty clear on what I was looking for in my next one; and I wasn't going to settle. Because of this, I hardly dated anyone for about a year...until I met Jennifer. She ended up being the office manager at the chiropractic office that my yoga instructor recommended to me; her sister and brother-in-law were the chiropractors. I remember two things about visiting that chiropractic office...

1. I saw Jennifer was wearing a ring on her wedding finger.

2. I was confused, yet pleasantly surprised when, after my initial appointment, Jennifer did a follow up call and asked me out to tea. It turned out she just liked to wear a lot of rings. ☺

Marriage. Probably part of the reason I was never in a long-term romantic relationship prior to being twenty-one years old was that, as far back as I can remember, nobody was ever good enough, and I was always looking at every female as potential marriage material. However, after a few dates with Jennifer, despite my critical eye, I couldn't find anything wrong with her; she was beautiful on both the outside and the inside. Ironically, as I was contemplating asking her to officially become my girlfriend, I remember saying to myself something that I never had before, "Just go into it and see what happens." What happened was, four months after we became an official couple, I proposed. A year and a half later we were married.

Teaching. By that time, I had started doing my thing; teaching public speaking and interpersonal communication classes part-time at a number of different colleges, including the college where I dreamt of teaching full-time. Although such full-time positions only opened up about once every fifteen years, not just one, but two positions happened to open up in the Communication Department at my dream school. Even though I had only been teaching about two years at that point and there were tons of highly qualified applicants from around the United States, I not only applied, but made it through the interview process to the final top four candidates. With two positions available, I had a really good shot at landing one of them. *Holy crap.* I began to see my life plan all mapped out in front of me; getting the job, having kids, and teaching until I retired into the sunset.

I don't know if you believe in fate, but my final interview was on my birthday. I thought it went well and I was told that I would be notified that evening, either way. It couldn't have been a better set up for a happy ending. After coming back from a baseball game that night with Jennifer, I came home to a message; a message that said I *didn't* get selected for one of the positions. I was, once again, acutely aware of the unknown.

Life. As I began to question the directionality of my career, while talking with a friend of mine one day, she handed me a business card and suggested that I contact the man on it. As it turned out, he was a Life Coach. After meeting with him and discussing more about what he did, I found out that he got paid really well to work with people on reaching their fullest potential in life. He also trained people to do what he did. About a year later, I signed up for his yearlong coaches training program and began to explore my life at a much deeper level than simply reading books.

College students. As a teacher, it's quite hard for me to learn something new and valuable and not want to share it with others. So, as I went through my coaches training program, although I typically coached older business executive clients, I found myself subtly implementing some coaching stuff into my classroom. Due to the fact that my public speaking and interpersonal communication courses were some of the most "life applicable" classes students could take, it wasn't too challenging to do. The challenging part was when I became drawn more and more to work with college students on <u>all</u> areas of life, not just their communication. And, because I was hired by colleges to teach communication courses, I wasn't able to do this as much as I would've liked. Because of this, it dawned on me to begin a private life coaching group for college students. When I first entertained the idea, I had an overwhelmingly positive response. One thing led to another and I began writing this book. Since then, based upon the material in this book, I've been speaking to students at colleges, holding weekend seminars for college students, and doing group and private coaching for college students.

Secret. *The 4 "Secrets" to College Life Success* that I'm about to share with you aren't anything new. A secret is nothing more than something that exists that you aren't aware of. Each one of these secrets already exists in your life. After reading this book, what I hope *will* be new is your awareness, because, the greater your awareness, the more powerful choices you can make in your life.

And, in order to support you in some of these choices, within each secret, I've not only included powerful information, but practical tools that I've learned, implemented, and taught for over a decade. I'm not even close to knowing everything about each secret, but my hope is that what I'm about to share will support you, in some way, in thriving in your life during and after college.

Clint Pardoe
December 31, 2010

SECRET #1

SELF-CARE

Introduction. If you were excited to get started and skipped over the *Introduction* chapter, please go back and allow me to introduce myself before you read any further. My intention is that it will support you in developing a better understanding of me, what I'm about to share, and yourself. If you already have or once you do, please read on…

Self-care. The common stereotype about college students is that they don't take very good care of themselves; they lack self-care. Unfortunately, having taught thousands of college students from all over the world, this stereotype seems to be pretty accurate. It's almost as though, included with all of the information students receive when they first enter college, they are given a "free pass" that gives them permission to not take good care of themselves for the rest of their educational experience. The degree to which college students neglect taking care of themselves, of course, varies, but it's pretty common that it occurs. However, because it's so common, so widely expected and accepted from both the college culture and the culture at large, many students aren't aware that another reality exists.

The reality. I'm going to give you three choices.

1. Self-Care
2. Relationships
3. School/Work

Out of these three choices, pick the one that usually takes precedence over everything else in your life; the one that is your primary focus as a college student. And, by the way, this is not a test. There is no right answer. There is no grade. So, please don't pick the one that you think is correct, but what is actually true for you. Simply take a moment to reflect on your life currently. Then, choose. And please only pick <u>one</u>; there is no "tie."

Got it?

Results. As I've already mentioned, if you're like most college students, you probably didn't choose number one; self-care. If this is true, and you chose something else, you are not wrong and you didn't fail. You're simply beginning to bring more awareness into this area of your life. After reading this chapter, you may or may not choose to put self-care at the forefront of your life but, because of your increased awareness, you will be able to make a more conscious and powerful choice about it.

If you did choose self-care, you are the minority. However, this is not a test. You are not right. And you don't get an "A." Your choice to put self-care at the forefront of your life has many great benefits. And, after reading this chapter, you may be aware that what you're currently doing to take care of yourself is exactly what you want to be doing or you might find that there's another level of self-care that you have never even considered.

Another reality. I've asked thousands of college students to name some of the most common ways in which they could take good care of themselves and the three quickest responses have always been exercise, sleep and nutrition. Although these answers are extremely common, taking good care of yourself can mean different things to different people; so I'd like to clarify what I mean by it.

Selves. While the three responses from students that I mentioned are great answers, they only pertain to nurturing one part of yourself; your **physical** self. In addition to your physical self, I invite you to consider that you have an **emotional**, **mental**, and **spiritual** part of yourself as well. And, that taking good care of yourself means nurturing all aspects of yourself; your "selves." With some borrowed examples from the most cutting-edge book on the subject matter, *Integral Life Practice: A 21st-Century Blueprint for Physical Health, Emotional Balance, Mental Clarity, and Spiritual Awakening* by Ken Wilber, Terry Patten, Adam Leonard, and Marco Morelli, the following is a brief description of each aspect of yourself as well as some things you can do to nurture it.

Physical. This part of yourself is pretty self-explanatory. Some ways to nurture your physical body include, but aren't limited to healthy nutrition, running, walking, lifting weights, swimming, tennis, chiropractic, acupuncture, hiking, aerobics, biking, dancing, martial arts, massage, pilates, yoga, surfing, kickboxing, wakeboarding, kayaking, rock climbing, rollerblading, sauna, hot tub, stretching, vitamins, organized sports, sleep, etc.

Emotional. Stereotypically, women tend to be in touch with their emotions more than men. However, everyone has a part of them that experiences emotions. Some ways to nurture your emotional self include, but aren't limited to spending time with people, taking a relationship class, counseling, acting, journaling, art, playing music, poetry, dancing, touch, screaming in a pillow, etc.

Mental. This is the intellectual part of yourself and is where college students spend most of their time. Some ways to nurture the mental part of yourself include, but aren't limited to reading, meaningful conversations, listening to a lecture, etc.

Spiritual. Depending on your belief system, or lack thereof, you may choose to connect with this part of yourself in different ways. Some ways to nurture your spiritual self include, but aren't limited to meditation, going to church, prayer, walking in nature, music, reading spiritual teachings, silence, solitude, volunteering, etc.

Top 4 list. One of the most powerful tools that I've recently begun to use both personally and with my coaching clients is a revised version of a well-being checklist originally taught to me by *Accomplishment Coaching*, the organization that initially trained me how to coach. I call it the "Top 4 list."

It's a list of the top 1−4 essential things that, if you did daily (typically M−F), would serve to nurture yourself? They don't have to be complex or even brand new things. Simply take into consideration <u>all</u> aspects of yourself and, in addition to being *essential*, make sure they are *specific* and *realistic*. Here are two examples of top 4 lists...

(Example #1)

1. Sleep 8 hours − **physical**
2. Healthy nutrition − **physical**
3. Exercise 45 minutes − **physical**

(Example #2)

1. Sleep 8 hours − **physical**
2. Hang out with friends for 1 hour − **emotional**
3. Reading 1 hour − **mental**
4. Meditation 20 minutes − **spiritual**

You'll notice that, in Example #2, there's not only more items, but there is more of a focus on multiple areas. Either way works. There may be times in your life where the number of things you do and/or the aspects of yourself that need the most attention are different. Simply being aware of the different aspects of yourself, as well as some things you can do to nurture them, will allow you to choose most powerfully. And, just because something is not on your top 4 list doesn't mean that certain aspects of yourself aren't being nurtured. The purpose of the list is to create awareness to the things that truly nurture the most important aspects of yourself so that you make sure to do them.

Tracking. Speaking of doing them, I encourage you to create your own top 4 list and either post it somewhere you can see it or keep it somewhere where you can easily access it. And, whether it's throughout the day or at the end of each day, consider tallying up how many of the 3 things you did. Then, at the end of each week, consider adding up all of the numbers and dividing them by the number of days you tracked. This will give you an average. Divide this number by the number of things on your list and it will give you a weekly percentage or "grade." Here's an example...

	M	T	W	TH	F
Sleep 8 hours	x		x	x	
Healthy nutrition	x	x	x	x	x
Exercise 45 minutes	x	x	x	x	
Total	3	2	3	3	1

3+2+3+3+1 = **12**

12/5 days tracked= **2.4**

2.4/3 items=**80% = "B-"**

Can you imagine getting graded on your self-care and having it be part of your overall GPA?

By doing all of this, you'll start to notice right away what you tend to nurture, what you tend to neglect and, more important than a grade, how your overall daily and weekly percentages make a difference in your life.

Nurture. When I was in college, I wasn't aware that I had different parts of myself that might need nurturing. I was, however, aware that I had a **physical** self. I used to lift weights and do some sort of cardiovascular workout for about 2 hours/day; and I would usually do this in addition to surfing, or even after a long day at work moving furniture. I was in really "good" shape. Then, after I began experiencing anxiety, I had some tests done on my heart. The doctors concluded that absolutely nothing was wrong with me physically; actually, I was really "healthy. "

For most people, being in good shape and healthy are optimal physical goals. So, what I was doing to take care of myself were probably the best choices for me, right? Not necessarily. When I started asking myself the question, "What truly nurtures me," I started to notice how I felt when I did these activities. For the most part, I felt like crap! **Physically**, I was sore most of the time; **emotionally**, I was tired a lot; and **mentally**, I could hardly concentrate unless I was taking lots of naps or drinking tons of coffee. My **spirit**, for the most part, seemed depleted.

Should. At my *College Life Success Boot Camp*, in addition to it being about taking action on the material in this book, since most college students have no idea about or experience with life coaching, I spend a section of the weekend coaching the participants on their goals and/or real life situations. I usually begin by asking the participants something like, "What would you like some coaching on?"

During the first *College Life Success Boot Camp* that I ever tried this out at, the initial response was complete silence. Eventually, one female participant raised her hand and said something like, "As college students, maybe we're so busy that we've never really taken the time to think about such a question?" I agreed with her and shared that, if need be, we'd spend the entire hour together in silence in order to give everyone an opportunity to see if anything arose. Shortly thereafter, students began to ask for some coaching.

I share this with you because, similarly, when it comes to the question "What truly nurtures you?" perhaps it's challenging to answer because students haven't really ever taken the time to think about it; or maybe they've just never been asked.

Whether you've been asked or not, the answer to what truly nurtures you might be an unconscious script that, like a computer application, has been downloaded into your hard drive. Whether it's from parents, friends, teachers, or the culture at large, many college students are used to being told things and, more often than not, these things become an unconscious *should*. Be careful of even taking my suggestions and turning them into another thing you should do. There's value in other people's opinion, but should is someone else's choice, not yours.

Choice. Donald Epstein, founder of Network Spinal Analysis, says, "A choice is most satisfying when it's your own." Whether it's lifting weights and doing some sort of cardiovascular workout for 2 hours/day or doing nothing, it's important to consider what's best for *you* when thinking about the things that nurture yourself. Depending on your body type, preferences, etc. your optimal choices may be very different from what everyone else does or what you are told you should do. What nurtures others or what others think best nurtures you, might not actually be what's best for you.

Mind. As you are considering all of this, be careful of your mind. Notice if you just said to yourself something like, "I just started doing a cardio workout 4 times/week for 30 minutes because I heard it would be good for me and I hate it, so I'm going to quit."

First of all, just because someone else suggests something to you doesn't mean it won't nurture you. And, even if you have an innate desire to nurture yourself in a certain manner, doesn't mean you're always going to like it. Sometimes people might not enjoy things at first because they don't want to put in the effort and they use "I don't like it" or "it's uncomfortable" as an excuse to not give it a whole-hearted try. Many people don't like the discomfort that comes with doing something new or different. However, despite some initial resistance, if people keep going, many times they may find that they really enjoy the thing they didn't like at first. So don't give up too easy. You might want to ask yourself, "Do I not want to do this because I don't want to deal with the initial discomfort, or do I not want to do this because it truly doesn't nurture me?" There's a difference.

After some honest effort (I recommend a solid 3 months), you may find that something really doesn't nurture you. If you truly don't enjoy something, explore what else you can do to in its place that might be more satisfying. And don't let yourself be fooled. Just because you may work through some initial resistance in the beginning, doesn't mean that there won't be more challenges to follow. Like life, you're probably not always going to enjoy it all of the time. And, whether you're enjoying it or not, taking good care of <u>all</u> aspects of yourself will affect <u>all</u> areas of your life.

All areas. At the beginning of this chapter, I gave you three choices (self-care, relationships, school/work) and asked you to pick the one that usually takes precedence over everything else in your life; the one that is your primary focus as a college student. While it could be argued that relationships or school/ work could be classified as taking care of yourself, as I hope you've learned by now, self-care is different. Self-care has nothing to do with putting relationships or school/work before yourself because they're important to you, but has everything to do with how these areas are affected by you taking really good care of yourself; because <u>all</u> are important to you.

Relationships. Most people agree that one of the biggest contributing factors to how they relate to other people is largely dependent upon their mood; and that their mood is greatly influenced by how well or not so well they take care of themselves.

SELF-CARE → MOOD → RELATIONSHIPS

It's not realistic to expect that taking good care of yourself will always make you feel good, or even that you should always feel good, but, whether it's with a romantic partner, friend, or family member, when you're in a better mood, you tend to perceive others in a more favorable light, be less reactive, and show up more fully.

17

School. Speaking of which, many students don't show up as fully as possible in school due to their lack of self-care. Something as simple as getting enough sleep can greatly influence a student's ability to participate and learn. After all, those things are hard to do when you're not awake. ☺

And, despite the average college student's youthful energy, not taking care of oneself can leave a student completely depleted. Just take a look around you during finals week. As a matter of fact, I dare you to end a quarter/semester as energized as you began it! It's totally possible. It's just a matter of whether or not you choose to take care of yourself consistently.

Consistency. If you don't consistently deposit money into your checking account and you go to the ATM machine everyday to withdraw money that you need, what's going to happen? At some point, it's not going to give you any! It's the same with self-care. Many students don't put consistent deposits into their self-care account and often feel overdrawn; like they don't have what they need. And then, at some point, they become completely overdrawn.

Just like your checking account, if you consistently put deposits into your self-care account, not only will you have the resources necessary for everyday life but, over an extended period of time, you will probably have built up enough reserves to cover any unexpected occurrences.

Vegas. Let's say that you consistently take good care of yourself. Then, one weekend, you spontaneously decide to go to Las Vegas with your friends. And, because it's Vegas, not only do you hardly sleep, but you neglect every other aspect of yourself. However, because your self-care account was full from your previous deposits, you had the resources to more effectively recover from your lack of self-care more than you would have if you didn't have anything in your account. Make sense? And, by the way, this doesn't give you an excuse to take good care of yourself throughout the week so that you can use up all of your resources on the weekend.

Rigidity. In addition to the extreme amount of exercise I used to partake in during college, I used to be very rigid with my diet. I would pay really close attention to labels on food and, if I ate out, I had numerous questions about ingredients that probably drove people nuts. However, once the weekend came around, I would go out drinking with my friends and end up eating tons of greasy food at one in the morning. I would restrict myself during the week and then indulge during the weekend. This wasn't very satisfying. Like exercise, it was only when I allowed myself to be flexible enough to eat what truly nurtured me, even if it was a scoop of ice cream in the middle of the week, I began to feel more satisfied.

Flexibility. When it comes to self-care, what's best for you at one point in your life may not be at another. Simply check in with yourself and see what's true for you. Choose what you sense is best for you now and see what works. If you are interested in your life being different from what most college students are used to, then commit to your self-care, yet be flexible within your commitment.

ACTIONS

1. Write down one major way that taking good care of yourself would effect your relationships and school/work.

2. On the lines below, list your top 1—4 *essential* things that, if you did daily, would best serve to nurture yourself. Remember to take into consideration all aspects of yourself (**physical, emotional, mental**, and **spiritual**) and make sure the items are *specific* and *realistic*.

   1._____

   2._____

   3._____

   4._____

3. Write or type the above top 4 list on a separate sheet of paper and, like in the example I previously used in the chapter, add Monday through Friday categories across the top right. Post it somewhere you can see it or keep it somewhere where you can easily access it. Begin tracking your overall daily and weekly percentages. Do this for at least one quarter.

SERVICE

*"Make sure your oxygen mask is on before assisting
other passengers."*

~Airline Safety Instructions

Selfish. Even if you are interested in your life being different from what most college students are used to and are committed to taking good care of yourself, you still might not. One of the possible reasons for this is that it might feel selfish. After all, many people are taught that putting themselves first is selfish and putting others first is selfless; and being selfless is more admirable. However, many people who are considered selfless put others first at the expense of themselves; and the people they serve.

It's like the ATM example I used before. If people give, give, give, without giving to themselves, then eventually they will have nothing left to give. And, in my opinion, that's selfish. The people they are supporting aren't always getting the best possible them. On the other hand, I'm not advocating that you become selfish and only take care of you for the sake of yourself. It doesn't have to be one extreme or the other. Self-care can actually be an act of service.

Service. While the act of serving others can be a way in which people take care of their spiritual selves, serving all aspects of yourself will not only benefit you, but can allow you to best serve others. From my experience, serving all aspects of myself allows me to more fully serve my wife, my kids, my friends, my family, and college students. This leads nicely into the second secret, which is all about relationships…

SECRET #2

HEALTHY RELATIONSHIPS

Learned. We interact with human beings every day. However, unless you major or minor in Communication Studies, it's highly unlikely that you'll be required to take a class on how to create healthy relationships in your life. And, unfortunately, we are not born with a set of instructions on how to do so. For the most part, how you relate to other people was learned from the person(s) who raised you. And do you think they were required to take a relationship class at some point in their education? Probably not. And where do you think they mostly learned how to relate to others? From the person(s) who raised them. Now, we're going way back. I'm talking about some of your grandparents, here. And do you think they were required to take such a class? I highly doubt it.

Unconscious. If you're like most people, I'll bet you've inherited some healthy ways of relating to others but, because the majority of people have never been required to take a course on it, you've probably inherited a lot of unhealthy ways, too. Either way, most people are *unconscious* when it comes to how they relate to others and this can be a recipe for a lot of unhealthy relationships. The good news is that, no matter what you've learned or how unconscious you are, you have the ability to create healthier relationships in your life.

Conscious. The goal of this chapter is to teach you some powerful communication skills so that you can play a *conscious* role in your relationships. Because, as a college student, you interact with people every day and, no matter how healthy or unhealthy your current relationships are, it's likely that you're missing out on what's actually possible in relationship with other human beings.

Warning! Just like if you choose to start taking better care of yourself, if, after reading this chapter, you decide to change some of the ways you communicate, *your decision will influence others in one way or another*. The common misconception is that if people choose to better their lives, everyone will be supportive. Not necessarily. My favorite comedian of all time, Mitch Hedberg, once said, "I played in a death metal band. People either loved us or they hated us or they thought we were ok." Similarly, when you choose to change, people will respond in one of three ways; they'll love it, hate it, or they'll simply be ok with it. No matter what the reaction, who you are and what you do will have an effect on others and contribute to what's possible in your relationships with other human beings.

BEING

"Be the change you wish to see in the world."

~Mahatma Gandhi

Being. Most researchers agree that about 93% of our communication is non-verbal; which means it doesn't involve talking. Therefore, when it comes to relationships, it's not only what you say but *how* you say it that's important. For example, you could say, "I love you," rudely or kindly. You are either *being* rude or *being* kind. *How* you say what you say is essentially who you are *being*. Many people are unaware of who they are being and the effects it has in relationship to other people.

Systems. Ok, I'm going to get a little theoretical on you, but I promise to keep it as simple as possible. As a matter of fact, what I'm about to share with you in <u>one sentence</u> is the culmination of about a year and a half of my life studying this theory as a focal point in graduate school. You're welcome. ☺

In a nutshell, systems theory states that, "Everything is interconnected and, because of this, a change in one thing produces a change in the rest, which produces a change in the system as a whole." When thinking about systems theory in the context of relationships, it can be translated into, "We are all interconnected and, because of this, a change in one person produces a change in other people, which produces a change in what happens." In other words, *you influence the person (s) and outcome (s) of every interaction.*

Believe it or not, I already shared a prime example of this theory as applied to relationships at the beginning of this chapter without you being aware of it. To refresh your memory, earlier I said…

"Just like if you choose to start taking better care of yourself, if, after reading this chapter, you decide to change some of the ways you communicate, *your decision will influence others in one way or another.*"

Now, let's take a look at how who you are *being* fits into this equation…

Waiting tables. If you've ever waited tables or currently do so, I have a lot of admiration for you. I did it on and off for six years during college and it's not easy. And, yes, I've had my fair share of waiting table nightmares. For those of you who have never waited tables, waiters will often have recurring dreams about not getting to their tables fast enough, orders getting messed up, customers yelling, etc. Many times these dreams occur after working a night shift and, if you work the following morning shift, it can feel as though you never left work.

Despite the challenges of the job and the occasional nightmares, as a college student, it was one of the easiest ways to make good money in a short amount of time; which, of course, was one of the biggest reasons I initially wanted to do it. Upon reflection, what I ended up learning was that it can also teach you a lot about communication.

Communication. The word communication is derived from the word commune, which means to come together; to connect. Although people communicate with each other, it doesn't always mean that they connect. On the contrary, when it comes to waiting tables, there's often a lack of connection between the server and the customer. Have you noticed this? This may be because, similar to me when I first began waiting tables, many servers are there to make the most money in the shortest amount of time. It may also partially be due to the way a customer stereotypically treats a server. When interacting with a server, often times a customer will treat them as means to an end as well. After all, the server is the person between them and their food; and that's about all the connection a customer is interested in. So, both a server and a customer communicate, but that doesn't necessarily mean that they connect. So what? Why would you want to connect with someone you hardly know anyway?

Connection. This question was prompted within me after reading a book called *The Celestine Prophecy* by James Redfield. Even though it was fictional, one of the things that the book discussed was that, whether meeting someone for the first time or running into someone you already knew, there was no coincidence. There was a deeper reason for it. And, if you were present, certain people had valuable information for you and the next direction of your life. Whether or not it was true, the idea was intriguing to me, and it led to a drastic change in my number one priority at work; to *connect* with my customers. I went into work excited about who I was about to get to know and, when interacting, I practiced being as present as possible with them.

Present. There are many things that can distract us from being present, or fully in the moment, in our lives. One of the biggest distractions is the thoughts that race around in our mind. Well, being as my main reasons for waiting tables had been to make good money in a short amount of time, guess what, in addition to remembering orders, I tended to think about while working? How much money I was making and what time I would get off. If you've ever worked before, you can probably relate to one or both of these thoughts while working. And, if you're like me, these recurring thoughts got in the way of me being able to be fully present with my customers.

So, in the spirit of being more present, I practiced being less and less interested in what my tips were going to be. I wouldn't even look at them until the very end of my shift when I was done. If you've waited tables before, you know how challenging that would be to do. For those of you who have never waited tables, you can probably guess what the very first thing most servers do after you leave your table; look at how much tip you gave them.

I also practiced being less and less interested in what time I was going to get off of work. I was there to serve people, to connect with them; however long it took. This didn't mean that I spent hours having in-depth conversations with each customer; after all, you can deeply connect with someone by simply looking at them. However, this might have been a little weird to my customers so, in addition to making eye contact, a quick way I initially connected with them was to simply ask how they were doing.

How are you? Probably the most common phrase out of a server's mouth as they approach a customer is, "How are you?" And, from my experience, just like in many other relationships, because it's a common cultural greeting, it's often asked very robotically.

Kind. Because of this awareness, combined with my intention to connect, when I asked a customer how they were doing, I practiced *being* kind; the type of kind that wasn't robotic, but actually demonstrated that I cared, on some level, about them and their experience.

Rude. However, there was the occasional customer who, when I attempted to connect with them by being kind, would say something like, "Coke with no ice and make it quick, I need to be out of here in twenty minutes." It wasn't even that they didn't acknowledge the fact that I asked them a question, nor was what they said necessarily rude, it was *how* they said it. They were *being* rude. I've had customers who would answer such a question, "Fine, thanks. I'll have…" and would *be* rude about it. Now, let's hit the pause button and do a little re-cap…

Re-cap. Systems theory, as applied to relationships, basically says that, "We are all interconnected and, because of this, a change in one person produces a change in another, which produces a change in the outcome of the interaction." In other words, *you influence the person (s) and outcome (s) of every interaction.* And, one of the biggest ways that you influence other people and what happens is by who you are *being.* In the above example, I was *being* kind and the customer was *being* rude. Make sense so far?

Automatic. When someone attempts to connect with another person by being kind and the other person is rude to them, what normally happens next? What do you think is the *automatic* reaction of most people? From my experience, they are rude right back. However, in a work environment, being rude back to a customer will probably get you into trouble so, more than likely, people will continue to be kind; robotically. It's like when you see someone you don't like and pretend to be nice to them. The interaction lacks authenticity.

Despite such a customer being rude, I would continue to practice being kind; genuinely. It wasn't that I was a doormat for people or that I didn't have any desire to be rude back, I simply, like my thoughts about making money or getting off of work, wasn't that interested in making it a focal point. This was very different from how most of my co-workers *automatically* reacted to such situations.

Extra. I worked with servers at restaurants who would take such an interaction very personally, would automatically put a smile on their face to the customer but, in the back, it was a whole different story. And, just in case you get sick to your stomach easily, I won't even begin to tell you about when I witnessed a server add a little something "extra" to their customer's order; and probably served it with a smile. And, just for the record, this happened at a pretty nice restaurant where you would never expect such a thing.

The little something "extra" that I served such customers was more kindness. After all, their rudeness probably had nothing to do with me. Maybe they just found out that their partner cheated on them? Maybe they lost their job that day? Or, maybe they were simply in a bad mood? Ever experience one of those? I don't know, maybe it was about me. Maybe they didn't like kind people? Or people with blonde hair? Who knows, and it didn't really matter. My intention was to connect with people and, if we were all interconnected, I wasn't going to *allow* one customer to ruin my shift.

The customer. This might be a little weird, but imagine being a customer at a restaurant and, at your table, there was a breathalyzer test; but instead of measuring your alcohol level, it measured your rudeness level. If one of these customers would have blown into the breathalyzer at the beginning of our interaction, on a scale from 1—10 with 10 being "extremely rude," the type of customer that I'm referring to would've probably scored about an 8.

However, by me continuing to be kind, often the customer's rudeness tended to lower throughout our interaction and a different part of them would emerge; they would start being kind back! They didn't skip out of the restaurant whistling but, by the end of their meal, they were about a 4 on the rudeness scale. Now, maybe this had a little to do with the fact that they got fed (my cousin gets really grouchy when he's hungry) but, I propose, it had just as much to do with how *who I was being influenced who they were being.* And, it also influenced the outcome of the interaction as well.

The outcome. More often than not, these customers and I would end up having a deeper conversation about each other's lives. As a matter of fact, many of these people would ask my name and eventually come back to the restaurant and request to sit in my section. On many nights, I would have an entire section filled with regular customers that I didn't previously know. Talk about connection!

And, ironically, despite me not focusing on my tips and thinking about what time I was going to get off of work, guess what happened as a result of all of this? I got the best tips ever and was having a great time working! I don't know that I met anyone that had valuable information for me and the next direction of my life, but I was more present…not waiting for some future event, like money or time, to make me happy. After all, life is NOW.

Relationship math. If this whole situation were a math equation, it would look something like…

Kind (Me)

+ Rude (Them)
= Kind (Them)
= Connection (Outcome)

Sounds utopian, right? You may be thinking to yourself, "All that I have to do is be kind to people when they're rude and then they'll end up being kind and we'll end up having an amazing connection!" Not necessarily. As I mentioned at the beginning of this chapter, your decision to better yourself and your relationships will influence others and, contrary to the example above, people won't always love it.

Drama. Do you know anyone that loves drama? People who look for opportunities to feed on it? They might be left hungry by your kindness and, like my cousin, grouchy until they are fed. So, if you do not give them any drama to eat, they will, like a person starving, do anything to try and engage you in a dramatic reaction. And, if you don't feed them, their rudeness may actually increase, producing a not so utopian outcome.

Kind (Me)
+ Rude (Them)
= Rude x 2 (Them)
= No Connection (Outcome)

Potential. Being genuinely kind, as you can see, can create two very different responses and outcomes. However, I'd like to remind you of something very important...

Being kind to someone who is rude can piss them off even more and <u>it can also open the space for them to be kind as well.</u>

Automatically reacting rudely back to someone who is rude can piss them off even more and it also closes off the space for them to be kind. I've never seen two people being rude to each other suddenly be kind. The outcome is predictable. Rude plus rude equals drama. However, being kind can create a *potentially* different response and a *potentially* different outcome. This can create an opening for others to be more powerful, for a different part of them to emerge that wouldn't have otherwise, and for an outcome to take place that may have never existed.

Always. The point of me sharing this with you isn't to preach that you should be genuinely kind all of the time to everyone. Being kind may be a worthwhile intention but, we're human beings, and it's not very realistic. Plus, there are many ways of being that we embody in our everyday interactions; kind and rude are just two examples of how we say what we say. But, the fact of the matter is that we are always being a certain way, we are always influencing others, and we are always influencing the outcomes of interactions. Most people are just doing it unconsciously.

Who are you being? So, I invite you to take a moment and reflect upon who you are currently being in certain relationships, what effect it might be having on the people involved, and how it may be influencing what is happening. How might you more powerfully show up?

Who are you being in your family?

Who are you being in your romantic relationship?

Who are you being with your close friends?

Who are you being with acquaintances such as teammates, classmates, teachers, co-workers, or the person who takes your food order?

Ripple. And, how does who you are being ripple out into the relationships that these people have with others and the outcomes that take place? For those of you who don't think that who you are being makes that big of a difference, I know of a few people that would probably disagree with you; Mahatma Gandhi, Dr. Martin Luther King, Mother Teresa, Cesar Chavez, The Dalai Lama, etc. All of them, human beings, just like you who, because of who they chose to be, powerfully influenced others and various outcomes. Your intention may not to be a world leader, but who you are being does make a difference.

In your everyday interactions, I invite you to begin to notice who you are being with people on a regular basis. This action alone is a huge step in becoming more responsible for the experiences in your relationships.

Actions

1. Begin noticing who you are *being* in interaction with others. Notice how it affects other people and various outcomes.

2. Practice being present with people at work. If you don't work, practice being present with people at school.

RESPONSIBILITY

"By accepting our responsibility as agents of our own life experience
we empower ourselves to make positive changes.
We hold the key to our own empowerment."

~Ellen Grace O'Brian

Responsibility. While there are many factors that determine what happens in your relationships, as we've discussed thus far, you are a significant one of them. While it's naïve to either take credit for everything that goes well in a relationship or to blame yourself for everything that goes wrong, you can accept responsibility for as much of it as possible.

According to *The Oxford American College Dictionary*, one of the definitions of responsibility is, "the opportunity or ability to act independently." While there are many opportunities in relationship with others to evoke a person's ability to act independently, they are often lost because most people can't take advantage of their ability; they have never been taught how to effectively communicate separate from what they learned. This unconscious dependency can lead to people feeling powerless.

Powerless. People who feel powerless in their relationships often suffer, blame others and/or feel stuck. They feel as though they don't have the power to choose to *be* or *do* something different in their relationships and so, instead, they usually just complain about them.

Complaining. While sometimes necessary and therapeutic, for the most part, simply complaining doesn't healthily support you or your relationships with others. Do you know how much energy people expend on constantly complaining about certain relationships? And, more than likely, these complaints play over and over in people's mind just as much, if not more, than they verbalize them. This can be exhausting. The funny thing is that many college students think that lack of sleep is the only thing that makes them tired. ☺

Make believe. Speaking of complaining, let's pretend like you have the following complaints about a family member, a romantic partner, a close friend, and an acquaintance. (If it helps, feel free to substitute the opposite sex in some of the following examples.)

1. "My mom is so controlling. Every time I talk to her, she always tells me what I should be doing or not doing."

2. "My boyfriend is unexpressive. He never opens up to me about his feelings."

3. "My best friend is a complete slob. He lives with me and doesn't even replace the toilet paper roll when it runs out."

4. "My teacher is really boring. All she does is lecture."

Mirror, mirror. First off, let me briefly say this. Many of the complaints we have about other people are often because they reflect back something that we don't like about ourselves; a certain way of being that we have a judgment about. Some simple questions someone may want to ask themselves regarding the above examples are...

1. Where am I being controlling?
2. Where am I being unexpressive?
3. Where am I being a slob?
4. Where am I being boring?

You may not always be able to relate your complaints about someone else to how you are being in your own life but, if you do, it can open up a whole new world of possibility that involves compassion for both you and the other person. This alone can sometimes alleviate a complaint about someone entirely.

Be. Since we've discussed that who you are being is a large part of communication, let's take a look at who you can be differently in response to a complaint that you have about someone. In order to do this, you need to consider how who you've been being might contribute to what you are complaining about. To better understand this, let's take a look at the first example...

"My mom is so controlling. Every time I talk to her, she always tells me what I should be doing or not doing."

It's difficult for someone to be controlling when there is nobody to control. So, if someone is being controlling, in this case, your mom, you might contribute to her being that way by being controllable. If this was your situation, maybe it would change by you being more powerful with your mom? Ironically, in order to *be* more powerful, there are many things that you can *do*.

Sandwich. In order to stay consistent with the food theme in the chapter thus far, one of the most powerful things you can do about a complaint is to sandwich it in-between an acknowledgment and a request.

ACKNOWLEDGMENT
COMPLAINT
REQUEST

"Mom, I'm really grateful that you care enough about me to call regularly and see how I'm doing. (*Acknowledgment*) However, I notice that every time we talk, I feel like you are always telling me what I should be doing or not doing. (*Complaint*) I know you mean well, but I'm an adult in college and I would appreciate it if you would please refrain from doing that." (*Request*)

Layering a complaint in such a way, as opposed to just complaining, provides the other person with a tangible action to take. And, as opposed to just starting out with the complaint, the initial acknowledgment decreases the chances that the person will be highly defensive; which will increase the chances of them not only hearing you, but taking the action. You request may or may not be met, but this way of dealing with a complaint is usually very different from what most people do; which is to *react, give-in,* or keep *quiet.*

React. People who react to such a situation tend to do so by letting the person have it the moment they have a complaint about them. Let's take a look at the second complaint example to further illustrate this...

"My boyfriend is unexpressive. He never opens up to me about his feelings."

If someone dealt with this complaint in a reactive manner, they might immediately say something like, "You are so shut down, numb and scared to let anyone into your life!" This approach tends to contribute to more reactivity from the other person and, well, you know how the rest goes. However, it can also further shut the other person down. Being threatening may be a contributing factor to the other person being unexpressive. Many people aren't willing to open up to someone unless they provide an environment conducive to doing so; by being safe.

Give-in. People who give-in might say something about their complaint to the other person by either making a request or reacting but, when it comes down to it, if nothing changes, they end up giving in against their own best interest. Let's look at the third complaint example...

"My best friend is a complete slob. He lives with me and doesn't even replace the toilet paper roll when it runs out."

After someone communicates this complaint, if the other person doesn't become more neat and organized, they usually will tend to clean up for them; or continue to, if they already have been doing so. After all, the other option is a messy place to live in. Once again, being the caretaker of the place may contribute to the other person being taken care of; or a slob.

Quiet. This one is pretty self-explanatory. Some people, no matter how much it bothers them, never say anything at all. But don't let their silence fool you, for they can be silent but deadly. Many of these people are like boiling tea kettles. They tend to be hyper-aware of what bothers them about you and will make mental notes in their mind each time you be the way or do the thing they have a complaint about. And, with each mental note, their boiling temperature begins to rise. They will either pretend as though everything's fine between you and them while they gradually seethe with more and more anger or, eventually, they might end up exploding. And, if the latter occurs, like a tea kettle when it hits the boiling point, the release of built up pressure exuded at you is usually as loud and annoying. To illustrate this, let's take a look at the fourth complaint example...

"My teacher is so boring. All she does is lecture."

Whether on the quarter or semester system, a student might have this complaint throughout an entire course and never say a word. Well, at least not to the teacher. People who keep quiet about such complaints aren't necessarily completely quiet. If you were like me in college, I would usually complain about this type of situation to my girlfriend, friends, classmates, parents, etc; <u>anyone</u> but the teacher.

And, because the teacher is unaware of the complaint, they have no idea that anything is even wrong! Therefore, nothing is going to change. Being quiet may contribute to the teacher being boring. And, even if a student decides to blast the professor in some sort of anonymous evaluation form at the end of the course or on some type of professor rating website (not that I've ever had that happen to me ☺), it doesn't do the student any good while they are in the class.

True story. As a teacher, I've had many students over the years complain to me that their other classes were boring because they weren't as interactive as one of my communication courses. While I could empathize with them because that was my experience as a college student as well, based upon what we've talked about so far, you can probably guess what some of my responses have been for them to consider...

Where are you being boring?

Who are you being in the class that's contributing to the teacher being boring or the students not being interactive? Do you ask questions, contribute to class discussions, or introduce yourself to people in the class?

Have you shared this with the teacher and made any requests?

I've often dared my students to take action on some of these things in such classes. And, out of the thousands of students I dared to do this, I can remember only a handful actually doing it and getting back to me with the results. But, every single one of my former students that actually took the time to both try it out and get back to me reported a drastic shift in not only their experience the class, but as a student as well. I have a hunch it had a little to do with them and being more responsible?

Vote. Depending upon the person and situation, I'll bet that you deal with the various complaints you have about others differently. However, I propose that there is a primary way that you automatically deal with the complaints you have in your relationships. And, if you're like the majority of human beings on the planet, you probably tend to react, give-in, or keep quiet. What I invite you to do right now is take a moment to reflect on which one of these three is the most common for you, even if it's only 51% of the time. No ties, and please just choose <u>one</u>. Got it?

Dare. I have a dare for you. I'm not a psychic but, if you tend to react, because it's the most common way that you deal with a complaint, I'll bet you recently went off on someone about something you didn't like about them or what they did. I dare you to contact them and apologize.

If you tend to give-in, I'll bet you recently gave in to someone against your own best interest. I dare you to bring it up again.

And, if you tend to keep quiet, because that's my tendency, I can almost guarantee that as you're reading this sentence, there's probably something about someone that's bothering you right now, but you haven't said anything. I dare you to say something.

Brain twister. Based upon what I just mentioned, you may think that reacting, giving in, or keeping quiet are very ineffective ways of dealing with complaints. In the spirit of this section, I'm willing to be partially responsible for that interpretation since the previous examples pointed out their ineffectiveness. Here's the brain twister; they can be very effective. If you unconsciously communicate in these ways then, yes, they can be extremely ineffective. However, if you are conscious about how you choose to use these different means of communication, then they can be just as powerful as the sandwich example I mentioned earlier.

Rewind. Let's go back to our very first complaint example…

"My mom is so controlling. Every time I talk to her, she always tells me what I should be doing or not doing."

You decided to speak to her about this and sandwich the complaint in-between an acknowledgment and a request; as I shared before, you said, "Mom, I'm really grateful that you care enough about me to call regularly and see how I'm doing. However, I notice that every time we talk, I feel like you are always telling me what I should be doing or not doing. I know you mean well, but I'm an adult in college and I would appreciate it if you would please refrain from doing that." After saying this, your mom apologized, said she understood, and told you that she wouldn't do it again. You thanked her and were completely blown away. You thought to yourself, "This stuff is like magic!"…until the next conversation, when she did it again.

But, instead of giving up, you decided to remind her about it,

"Hey Mom, remember how I mentioned last time about you telling me what I should or shouldn't be doing…please don't do that." After this reminder, your mom was overly apologetic, said she forgot, and swore that she wouldn't do it any longer. You walked away from the conversation feeling good about the fact that you mentioned it again and how your mom responded; until the next time you talked to her, when she did it yet again.

Sometimes, like in this example, it may be more effective to react and let someone have it; especially, if, after many attempts, they keep doing the same thing over and over again. You might say something like, "Mom, enough! I'm an adult!" This may be exactly what needs to happen in order for things to change. Have you ever needed a good kick in the butt by someone in order for you to finally do something different? I know I have. It may be the very thing that someone else needs as well. This doesn't mean that it gives you permission to go around flipping out on everyone. Simply be aware when it may be a useful approach.

Letting go. Another way of looking at giving in is that, in some instances, it may be most powerful for you to let the situation go after you've said something and your own best interest hasn't been met. You may realize that, after your initial communication, the complaint isn't as important to you anymore. Or, it might be more powerful for you to put your own personal interest aside and allow someone else to and be a certain way or do a certain thing. Simply be aware not to use these ideas to help perpetuate a possible unhealthy pattern for you and/or the other person.

Silence. Finally, sometimes it might be most powerful for you to shut up and keep quiet. Have you ever said something and, in retrospect, wish you wouldn't have? Sometimes it's not appropriate to say something to someone. And, similar to giving in, keeping quiet might be more powerful because you may realize that your complaint really isn't that big of a deal. Simply be aware of the tendency to convince yourself that something isn't a big deal so that you don't have to say anything.

Listening. Speaking of silence, one of the most powerful things you can do when someone has a complaint about you is to simply listen; and shutting up doesn't mean shutting down. Actually, it's quite the opposite; listening is about you being present and alert.

Effortless. Contrary to popular belief, listening to someone doesn't take a lot of effort. As a matter of fact, being present and alert is effortless. What takes effort are all of the things that we do to avoid listening to someone; such as thinking about something else while they are speaking.

The next time you are listening to someone such as your mom, your romantic partner, your best friend, or your teacher, simply notice when you begin thinking about something else. Notice how your thoughts take you away from being present and alert. This simple act of noticing will effortlessly bring you right back to the present moment where true listening resides. This can be one of the greatest gifts you give people; your present and alert attention. And, sometimes, this is all it takes for the complaint to be resolved. You don't even have to say anything. Many people simply want to be listened to fully and completely.

Responsible responding. While silence in and of itself can be powerful, it's also important to consider, when appropriate, what to say in response to a complaint. Although there are many effective ways to verbally respond, since we've been talking about responsibility, one of the most powerful things you can do in response to a complaint is to acknowledge any responsibility on your part. Similar to the sandwich method, it can be useful to sandwich your responsibility in-between an apology and your commitment.

APOLOGIZE
RESPONSIBILITY
COMMITMENT

One of the complaints that my wife Jennifer has communicated to me before has been about how I don't help out with our kids as much as she would like me to; sometimes she feels like she has to do it all alone. After initially being reactive, I began to think about how I might play a role in the complaint and, after further contemplation, I responsibility responded with something like...

"I apologize." (*Apology*) "I realize that I'm so used to you taking care of the kids during the day while I'm working that, when I end my work day, it's easy for me to allow you to continue being the only parent. I can see how this would leave you feeling like you have to do it all alone." (*Responsibility*) "You can count on me to step it up." (*Commitment*)

This may take some reflection and practice, but it can work really well; especially if you genuinely understand the person's frustration, your role in the complaint, and have a heartfelt commitment to making a change.

Request. When you have a complaint about someone it can be useful to make a request of them and, when someone has a complaint about you, a simple, yet often very effective tool is to ask, "What's your request?" More often than not, this, in addition to responsible responding, will throw people off. When verbalizing a complaint, people are more than used to others reacting or shutting down. So, when you ask someone if they have a request about their complaint, it puts the responsibility in their hands to come up with something they would like you to do about it. If they can't, there's not much left to complain about. If they can, and you're willing to do it, there is no more complaint.

Responsible relationships. In relationships, being responsible means that, through the awareness of who you are being and what you are doing, you have the ability to take powerful actions that will increase the chances of them going well. However, even when things are going well in a relationship, many people tend to focus on the things that aren't.

Actions

1. Pick one person in your life and write down <u>all</u> of the complaints you have about them. For <u>each</u> complaint, ask yourself the following questions...

    A. Am I ever this way or do I ever do what they're doing?

    B. Who am I being in the relationship that might contribute to who this person is being and/ or what they are doing?

    C. Do I have a request? If so, consider using the sandwich method (Acknowledgment, Complaint, Request). If not, consider not complaining.

2. What is your automatic way of dealing with a complaint? Do you tend to react, give-in, or keep quiet? Because this is your tendency, you more than likely enacted this recently. If this is true, I invite you to address the person with whom this occurred. If you reacted, consider apologizing. If you gave-in, consider bringing what you wanted back up. If you kept quiet, then consider talking about it using the sandwich method.

3. Notice when you're not listening in conversations. Just notice.

4. The next time someone has a complaint about you, practice responsible responding (Apologize, Responsibility, Commitment) or ask them, "What's your request?"

PERCEPTION

"At any given moment 80 percent of a relationship is working and 20 percent is not. We tend to focus on the 20 percent and neglect the 80 percent."

~Randy Fujishin

Perception. It's been said that what we focus on becomes our reality. If you tend to focus on the 80 percent of a relationship that's working, your perception of the relationship will probably be that's it is going well. On the other hand, if you tend to focus on the 20 percent of the relationship that's not working, your perception will more than likely be that's it is not going well. When it comes to relationships, often times, our perception isn't always *the* reality, just our own. How we perceive who people are, what's working or not, and what people say or don't say, whether correct or incorrect, greatly affects how we interact with others and, ultimately, whether or not the majority of our relationships are, indeed, going well.

Human being. Because we're human beings, we all possess some great qualities and some not so great qualities; sometimes I can be kind and sometimes I can be rude. While you might be able to relate to this personally, you've also probably noticed a similar dual nature about other people as well? Well, maybe not at first.

Fairy-tale. While it can occur in any type of relationship, there's a period of time during the beginning of a romantic relationship when everything is usually very new and exciting. During this time period, the tendency is for someone to only see the other person's great qualities and either downplay or overlook their not so great qualities. However, whether it's a month or a year later, it's only a matter of time before they discover that this person is just a human being; and those not so great qualities become more prevalent in the relationship.

When this occurs, often times, people will perceive this as though the relationship isn't working and, perhaps because romantic relationships are often glamorized in our culture in a fairy tale-like way, if you were like me in college, many students will choose to end it at that point. Then, of course, they eventually end up meeting someone new and exciting, and the same thing happens. People can spend their entire lives moving from relationship to relationship searching for that one person who will be great all of the time. And, of course, because we're human beings, it is a fairy-tale.

Roles. Another common way in which we tend to see others is as the roles they play. For example, have you ever noticed how differently students act around a professor than a friend? From my experience, many students get all "professional" around a professor because of their title. It's pretty funny to witness. While this is totally normal, I'm curious what would happen if people dropped most of their role perceptions and simply saw people as human beings? If you were able to do this, who might you be and what might you do differently in your interactions?

Jose. My favorite type of food is Mexican and, conveniently, I live a few miles away from one of my favorite places to eat. Like most taquerias, it has tables where you can sit and eat your meal, but you need to order from someone at a register. When the place first opened up, I ate there at least a few times per week and, after a few weeks, I began to notice that the same guy took my order every time. Like most stereotypical food ordering scenarios, our interactions went something like...

"Hi."

"Hi."

"Can I take your order?"

"Yes, I would like a bean burrito, side of guacamole, and a small soda."

"For here or to go?"

"For here."

"Seven forty-three."

"Thank you."

"Thank you."

However, one day, in the spirit of relating to others as human beings, I decided to ask him his name. He replied, "Jose." And, I, of course, introduced myself. From then on, in addition to the ordering conversation that needed to take place, despite the fact that he didn't speak very good English and I didn't speak very good Spanish, Jose and I began to get to know each other. I eventually ended up introducing him to Jennifer and he introduced me to the rest of the staff; the more we ate there, the more it felt like our friends ran the place.

About a year later, Jose shared with me that he would be moving back to Mexico to be with his family; and he wouldn't be returning. As silly as it may seem, I actually felt sad about it. Who would take my order? In appreciation of the relationship we had developed over the register counter, I decided to find out when his last night working was so that I could not only say good-bye, but bring him a going away present. Ironically, the night I went in, before I handed him his gift, he ended up paying for my dinner. I was moved. I still remember the connection I felt with him as I accepted his gift, gave him mine, and we said our good-byes.

Happily ever after. Believe it or not, after about a year of being gone, Jose ended up moving back from Mexico and began working at the taqueria again; along with his new wife! Since then, both of our families have added kids to our lives and to our conversations. My daughter Coral and my son Curren are usually excited to go to what they call, "Jose's burrito place" and can be seen giving Jose and the rest of the staff high-fives upon their weekly arrival and departure… all because I chose to see Jose as a person instead of an order-taker.

Hot or not? Whether it's a quality someone possesses or a role someone is playing, what you notice about someone may be completely different from what someone else does. Have you and a friend ever met someone for the first time together at somewhere like school or a party and, after meeting them, one of you thought they were hot and the other person thought that they weren't so hot? You were both talking to the same person, but each of you had different perceptions about them? Just as two people can have different perceptions about the same person, two people can have very different perceptions about how a relationship is going.

Working/not working? Whether it's a family member, romantic partner, close friend, or acquaintance, many people have no idea what's working or not working in their relationship. Let me take that back. They have an idea, but they usually don't *know* what's working or not. Why? Because many people don't communicate about it; they don't clarify their own perceptions. How often do you think people have a specific conversation with someone in their life about what's working or not working in their relationship? In my experience, it hardly ever happens. Of course, I didn't do this as a college student either but, since then, I make an effort to have this conversation on a <u>regular basis</u> with at least my wife. What do I mean by "regular basis?" Good question. Because people's perceptions not only can be different about who someone is and what's working or not, but what someone says.

Words. To answer the question above, my wife and I have a conversation about what's working and not working in our relationship about once per week, usually at some point during our date night on Fridays; which I highly recommend having if you get married, have kids, and are interested in maintaining a healthy relationship with your partner. However, you don't have to be married with kids to have this conversation; you can have it with anyone that you're in a relationship with who is important to you. Just make sure, like the above example about "regular basis," that in your conversations, you practice clarifying your perceptions about what someone says; because the words they use might not always mean what you think.

Loving. Let's pretend that Jennifer and I are out on one of our dates and, while eating dinner, part of our conversation is about what's working and not working in our relationship. During the conversation, she mentions that she's not feeling very loved by me the past few days. And, instead of her complaining about it for most of our meal, she uses one of the tools I mentioned before and decides to simply request that I be more "loving." And, instead of me defending myself for the rest of our meal by pointing out all of the ways I feel that I have been loving, I decide to respond responsibly. I apologize to her that she's been feeling that way, communicate that I'm probably partially responsible for it because I've been working a lot the past week, and commit to being more loving the following week. She thanks me for listening, validating her feelings, and being willing to do something different. End of conversation.

Brilliance. So, I have this brilliant idea, I think. In the spirit of being more loving, the very next day I decide to surprise Jennifer with a dozen long-stem roses; the nice kind that cost around $50...baby's breath and all. There's a flower shop down the street from our house so, the next morning before I leave for work, I go to the flower shop, buy the roses, and put them on our kitchen table; all before she wakes up.

I drive to work that day thinking how brilliant I am! Excited to hear about how delighted she was by my surprise, I anxiously await for a phone call from her telling me how much she loved the roses. However, the day goes by and I receive no phone call. Because of my busy day, I actually forget about it, but am quickly reminded when I get home and see the roses sitting there as we eat dinner together. She still doesn't say anything. I end up going to bed a little disappointed, but take into consideration that she's had a busy day with the kids and trust that she'll remember to thank me the next day. And to make sure this happens, I decide to buy her another dozen the next day. And, yes, that's $100 in roses! Certain ways we choose to express love can be expensive.

Despite my valiant efforts, the next day she still doesn't say anything; and neither do I. I start to notice that, like a tea kettle, I begin to get upset, but I'm not going to stoop so low as to say anything about it. After all, I should give love without expecting anything in return, right? That evening, as we're sitting at the kitchen table eating dinner, barely able to see each other or our kids due to the 24 roses right in front of us, she finally says, "You know how I asked you to be more loving to me the other day?"

"Yes," I respond as I think to myself, "Finally, here is the acknowledgment for a job well done...it's about time!"

She continues, "When are you going to start working on that?"

In shock, I immediately blow up and say, "I'm sorry, I can't hear you due to the abundance of roses that are on the table!!!"

She quickly responds by saying, "Oh, yeah. I'm so sorry. I've been meaning to thank you for those, but I've just been so overwhelmed with the kids this week. They're beautiful. Thank you. But, if that's what you thought I meant by being more loving, it's not."

Then I ask a simple question that, if asked during our initial conversation, would have saved me time, money, and upset; "How would you like me to be more loving?"

"By telling me that you love me at least once per day," she replies.

Love language. People not only have different interpretations of what the word love means, but they also have different ways that they express and feel most loved. As a matter of fact, there's a book called *The Five Love Languages* by Gary Chapman that, according to him, describes five primary ways people express and interpret love.

1. Words of Affirmation
2. Quality Time
3. Receiving Gifts
4. Acts of Service
5. Physical Touch

...and I'll scratch yours. From my experience, do you know what people usually do in relationships when it comes to loving another person? They show their love for others in the way that they want to feel most loved. They think that their perception of what it means to feel loved is how others want to be loved. And, that's usually not the case. Just because you love your back being scratched, doesn't mean someone else will, too.

Growth. For example, Jennifer's primary love language is receiving gifts and mine is quality time. It's much more natural for Jennifer to be generous with me than to give me her undivided attention; and vice versa. Working as a marriage counselor, Gary Chapman also discovered that, for whatever reason, people are usually drawn to those who speak a different love language than their own. My sense is that it has something to do with the fact that it's extremely challenging to fulfill another person's love language; especially someone who you love the most. And, it's the challenge of our own growth that is at the heart of any meaningful relationship. As Eckhart Tolle, author of the best-selling book *The Power of Now* states, "Relationships aren't here to make you happy, they are here to make you more conscious."

To me, being generous with Jennifer requires that I put aside my tendency to be selfish. For her, spending quality time with me requires that she trusts Coral and Curren will be fine without her and, when she's with me, challenges her ability to be present. Without clarifying how each of us felt most loved, none of this would be known and, without it being known, we wouldn't be able to work on it.

Clarification. Speaking of clarification, if you had to choose one of the five love languages that made you feel most loved, what would you pick? What do you think other people in your life would pick? How would you know what they would pick? Maybe by simply sharing with them the five love languages and asking, "How do you feel most loved?" It sounds simple, but many people are too embarrassed to ask. After all, aren't you expected to know this stuff? Unfortunately, unless you have psychic abilities, probably the only way you will find out how to better love someone or what they meant by something they said is through clarification. The same is true for what someone doesn't say, or non-verbal communication.

Dating. Being as 93% of our communication is non-verbal, there are more than enough opportunities for things to be falsely interpreted. For example, let's say that you went out on a first date with someone. You really enjoyed it and, despite wanting to contact them the very next day, you played it cool and contacted them a few days later. Despite the multiple ways that you could've chosen to make contact, you decided to do it the old fashioned way; you called. Before dialing, you took a deep breath. As the phone rang, part of you hoped that their voicemail would come on and, as luck would have it, it did. Relieved, you left a message and told them to give you a call back when they had a chance. However, you didn't hear back from them that day or the next or the next...what are some possible perceptions you might have about them not calling you back? Maybe they didn't like you? Maybe they've been really busy? Maybe they're sick? Maybe, maybe, maybe...How would you know? Ask!!!

Non-verbal clarification. Whether someone rolls their eyes at you, wears a certain outfit, is late, changes their room décor, is quiet, etc. there is a simple tool that can help you to clarify non-verbal communication situations such as this.

OBSERVATION
CLARIFICATION

"I called and left a message for you the other day and noticed that you haven't called me back." (*Observation*) "Just curious what's up?" (*Clarification*)

Your perception of the situation may or not be true, but this simple conversation will allow you to actually find out as opposed to assume. Often times in this scenario, whether it's with a romantic interest or someone else in their life, people assume the worst and, because of such assumptions, will either give up on pursuing a new relationship or completely end an old one.

Final clarification. While 80 percent of a normal relationship is usually working, many of these tools are for the 20 percent that is not; because it's not useful to only focus on the 80 percent that is working and deny things that aren't. Only by being aware of what's not working and having some effective tools to deal with such things, will you increase the chances of your relationship working even more. However, this doesn't mean that you shouldn't be aware of or continue to work on the 80 percent of the relationship that is working. This needs attention, too, and one of the most powerful ways to focus on what's working well in your relationships is to practice acknowledgment.

ACTIONS

1. Pick one person in your life who you tend to notice their not so great qualities way more than their great ones. Practice focusing on their great ones and see what happens.

2. Practice treating others as human beings; no matter what role they play in life.

3. Pick someone in your life that you are close to. Consider asking them what's working/not working in your relationship. If, during the conversation, you are unclear about something that is being said, practice clarifying your perception.

4. Pick one person in your life that you would like to deepen your experience of love with. Consider sharing about *The Five Love Languages*, your love language, and ask about theirs.

5. Practice using the non-verbal clarification method (Observation, Clarification).

Acknowledgment

"People want to be seen, heard, and acknowledged."

~Hans Phillips

Acknowledgment. Even if people are aware of what's working in a relationship, they don't always communicate it; people will assume such things are known, that they are a given. It's this type of assumption that can lead to things not working so well because, unless the other person is psychic, they will not know until they are told. Verbal acknowledgment not only makes such things known, but reinforces things about a relationship that contributes to it continuing to work well. Although there are many ways to acknowledge someone, three of the most common are how someone looks ("You have such beautiful eyes"), what a person has done ("Thanks for helping me study for the exam"), and for who a person is ("You are incredibly kind"). I encourage you to start acknowledging people more, and if you already do it pretty regularly, I invite you to do it on a deeper level. Have you ever sat down and told someone everything that you loved about them?

What I love about you. When Jennifer and I were first dating, we celebrated her birthday at her sister's house. It was a stereotypical birthday party; food, singing, cake, ice cream, and presents. However, after she opened up her presents, her sister said, "Ok, it's time to tell Jenn what we love about her."

"What?" I said curiously.

"A few birthdays ago, after Jenn opened up her presents, we were all sitting around and I decided to suggest that we tell her what we love about her. It just came to me." explained her sister. "Since then, we do it for everyone on their birthday."

"Wow," I replied, as I began to feel my heart racing.

There I was, in a relatively new relationship with Jennifer, and I was about to tell her what I loved about her, in detail, in front of her entire family? Ironically, at the time, I was in graduate school studying interpersonal communication and was totally nervous. But, for the next half hour, each person, even me, despite the trembling in my body and nervous shaking in my voice, went around and shared what we loved about Jennifer; even her sister's children, who were barely old enough to talk. I was blown away. It was a really beautiful experience.

I was so touched by it all that the next time there was a birthday celebration in my family, after the gifts were opened and everyone was sitting around, I decided to share what Jennifer's family did and proposed that we try it out. While my family, unlike some families, often verbalized the words "I love you," I don't ever remember expressing it in this way; especially with my uncle, whose birthday it was. Everyone in my family not only liked the idea, but decided to participate. It didn't take long before the tears began streaming and tissues were being passed around.

Once we were finished, my grandma had something else to add. Currently, my grandma is 83 years old; although she might tell you differently. When I was in 5th grade, I chose to interview her for a report and she told me she was 47 which, if you do the math, doesn't add up at all. ☺ Even though she is 83 years old, she probably has more energy and zest for life than most 47 year olds; maybe more than most college students. This is one of the things that I love most about her. And, she's pretty funny, too. I had never told her these things directly until, after we shared with my uncle what we loved about him, my grandma suggested, that since her birthday had just passed, we tell her as well!

Living in peace. One thing led to another and a few hours later, we had gone around the room and shared with everyone in our family what we loved about them. It was a deeply moving experience for everyone. I remember thinking to myself how cool it must have been for my grandparents to not only hear what their children and grandchildren loved about them and each other, but for them to have verbalized their love in this way to everyone in their family. I'm pretty clear that if they would've died that night, they would've died in peace. More often than not, it takes a person being on their deathbed for them to share in this way; so they can die in peace. The good news is that you don't have to be on your deathbed to tell the people in your life what you love about them. You can share this with them now, before you or they die; so that you can live in peace.

I began to look forward to the acknowledgment part of my family's birthday parties more than anything and, when it was my birthday, despite being excited about it, I realized how receiving acknowledgement can be just as nerve wracking as giving it.

Acknowledgment Judo. In my experience, when it comes to people receiving acknowledgment, they usually do some form of what I like to call *acknowledgment judo*. Like a martial arts master who is being attacked, people will deflect acknowledgment and, if necessary, strike back.

For example, someone might acknowledge your eyes and you suddenly find yourself deflecting it by saying, "Really?

They are so plain; I wish I would've gotten my sister's...blah, blah, blah." Even in some instances where people appear as though they are accepting the acknowledgment by simply saying, "Thank you," the inside of their head will say something like, "They're just saying that because they probably want something from me." Or, people might strike back by saying, "Thanks, and I really love your eyes, too." Either way, due to some type of resistance, people don't fully take in the acknowledgment.

Resistance. In addition to mental resistance to acknowledgment, as I mentioned in the previous chapter, you have three other aspects of yourself; physical, emotional, and spiritual. As if your mind weren't enough, all of these parts of you can resist being acknowledged as well. Physically, your body may be tense or guarded. Emotionally, you may feel nothing. Spiritually, you may sense a disconnection or separateness from the person.

Here's the funny thing; when people acknowledge you, you're not being attacked. Maybe attacked by love. And why resist love? If you weren't resisting, what would you be doing? Consider you might be allowing.

Allowing. As simple as it sounds, as I mentioned before, the most basic thing you can do when someone acknowledges you is to just say, "Thank you." That's it. If that's the only thing you ever did differently, it would probably make a huge difference for you. However, if you're interested in how the other parts of yourself might be more receptive to acknowledgment, there are a few things you can do to practice allowing it. Physically, you can relax your body and allow yourself to breathe it in. Emotionally, you can allow yourself to feel the love behind the acknowledgment. Spiritually, you can allow yourself to be connected to the person.

If you notice that you can't practice these things because you don't get acknowledged that much, you can always ask for it!

Requesting acknowledgment. Ask for acknowledgment? How egotistical, right? Not necessarily. At the very beginning of this section, I mentioned how often times, even when people are aware of what's working in a relationship, they don't verbally acknowledge it. Because of this, there are times when you might need to ask someone to acknowledge you.

I think most people would agree that, no matter how much they resist giving or receiving it, acknowledgment ultimately feels good. Just this morning, before sitting down to write, I was feeling crappy. So, I decided to ask Jennifer if she would acknowledge me for all of the effort that I've been putting into this book. She did and it felt really good. I'll be honest, it didn't make my day, but it did help jump start my day of writing. The alternative was to wallow in my crap, hope that Jennifer would pull me aside sometime today and acknowledge me for what I've been doing and, if not, become resentful.

Requesting acknowledgment is just another way of you playing a significant role in your relationship experience as opposed to being at the effect of it. And, worst case scenario, if you ask someone for acknowledgment and someone says no, you can always acknowledge yourself. Even if someone says yes to your request, acknowledging yourself from time to time is not a bad idea.

Self-acknowledgment. If it's true that about 80 percent of a relationship is already going well, I'll bet that you have played a significant role in helping to create that in many of your relationships. Who have you already been being and what have you already been doing that has had them go so well? I invite you to take a moment, right now, and think of one thing that, because of who you've been being or what you've been doing, has had one of your current relationships go well.

Got it?

Now, I invite you to take another moment and acknowledge yourself...however that feels appropriate. A little self-acknowledgment from time to time may actually be the most significant component to you experiencing healthy relationships. Your ability to acknowledge both the great and not so great qualities about yourself will, in turn, allow you more fully accept other people in your life.

ACTIONS

1. Pick one person in your life and acknowledge them for at least one of the following; how they look, what they've done, or who they are.

2. Pick one person who you love a lot, but haven't necessarily shared, in-depth, what you love about them. For their birthday, consider sharing everything; or, why wait...do it now!

3. Notice when you resist when someone acknowledges you. Practice allowing it in.

4. Pick one person in your life that you don't feel acknowledged by. Request acknowledgment from that person.

5. Practice acknowledging both the great things and not so great things about yourself.

SIMPLICITY

"Maintaining a complicated life is a great way
to avoid changing it."

~Elaine St. James

Simplicity. Relationships are very complex, yet they don't have to be complicated. However, making things complicated is a great way to avoid having to *be* or *do* more. If you feed off of drama, then you don't have to be more powerful. If you complain about others and blame them, then you don't have to be more responsible. If you only see people's great qualities, then you don't have to deal with their not so great ones. If you only see people's not so great qualities, then you don't have to deal with their great ones. If you just treat people as their roles, you might miss their humanity. If you don't know what's not working or how someone feels most loved, then you don't have to step it up. If you live in fantasyland, then you don't have to deal with what's actually going on. If you don't acknowledge what's working well, then you don't have to be intimate. And, if you don't acknowledge yourself, you don't have to deal with your own greatness.

Leader. Deepak Chopra wrote a book entitled *The Path to Love* and, similar to the path to healthy relationships, it begins with you. *You* can powerfully influence the person and outcome of every interaction. *You* can be responsible for who you are being and what you do. *You* can see others greatness, forgive their humanity, and treat them beyond the role that they play. *You* can clarify what people say or don't say. *You* can acknowledge others as well as yourself. *You* can choose to be the leader of your relationships…just like you can choose to be the leader of your life in the areas of time management, money, environment, and goal-setting. This leads (no pun intended) nicely into the next secret...

SECRET #3
CREATIVE STRUCTURE

Homework. At some point in your education, I would bet that you've been given instructions about assignments that were very vague while others were extremely detailed. Which did you like the best? Maybe you're saying to yourself, "I don't like *any* type of homework." I understand, but I propose that you do have a preference when it comes to the above; not just about homework, but life in general. Perhaps you enjoy the freedom to be creative without someone telling you what to do? Or, maybe you like the organized structure of being told exactly what to do? Which one is it for you? Are you more creative or structured?

Creative/structure. The good news about people who are more creative, because they get to choose what to do, is that they tend to be more satisfied than people who are structured. However, the not so good news is that, because of their desire for freedom, they tend to not be as productive. On the other hand, the good news about people who are more structured, because they know exactly what to do, is that they tend to be more productive than people who are creative. However, the not so good news is that, because they tend to treat life like a checklist of things "to do," they tend to not be as satisfied. Any moment of satisfaction is usually attributed to something getting done and these moments are very brief; after all, there is always something to do. ☺

Both/and. As you can see, whether someone is more creative or structured, each has beneficial and not so beneficial aspects. What most people aren't aware of is that it's possible to receive the benefits of both. The goal of this chapter is to share with you how you can be both creative *and* structured within the areas of time management, money, environment, and goal setting, such that it will increase your chances of being both satisfied *and* productive.

TIME MANAGEMENT

*"Be assured that you'll always have time for the
things you put first."*

~Liane Steele

Time. There are only 24 hours in a day, 7 days in a week, and 52 weeks in a year. Although you may wish that you had more time, it's not going to happen. Many college students, due to their busy schedules, feel as though they don't *have* enough time. However, I invite you to consider that what you do with your time is a *choice*; that you have time for the things you put first.

Most important? If you want a quick glimpse into what things are most important to you in your life, simply take a look at how you currently spend your time. Despite you saying that something's important, if you're not making time for it, then it's probably not as important as you think. And, if you are doing things that aren't most important to you, then why are you making time for them? You don't have to do anything; even go to college.

College. You may be thinking, "I have to go to college if I want to be successful." No you don't. Do you know that some of the most successful people in the world never went to college? Look, I'm not advocating dropping out of college, but I don't think it's for everyone. And your success in life is not dependent upon it. This might be weird coming from someone who has gone to graduate school, taught college, and whose career is focused on supporting college students, but I've witnessed far too many students suffer because they feel as though they have to go to college rather than because they want to. I'm not saying that there aren't going to be days, weeks, or even months where you feel as though you don't want to go to school; that's normal. But you don't *have* to go.

Whether you're currently in school because you feel as though you have to or because you want to, be careful of thinking that how you manage your time will be fundamentally different at some point in the future.

Graduate school. I started dating Jennifer when I was in graduate school. We went out about once per month. She wanted to go out more, but I was too "busy" with school and told her that I didn't have time for a committed romantic relationship; as if I was going to magically *have* more time open up in my life after school. Upon reflection, one of the reasons I didn't *make* the time for a committed romantic relationship with Jennifer was because, like many college students do, I used time to avoid being in a relationship that would require more of me than I was willing to give.

As I mentioned before, although challenging, romantic relationships can serve as one of the most powerful vehicles for you to reach your fullest potential as a human being; even in college. If you truly aren't interested in being in a romantic relationship, that's fine. However, if you are interested in being in a romantic relationship or are currently in one, I encourage you to make time for it now (while being careful of using your romantic relationship to avoid things like school) as opposed to waiting for something, like more time, to open up in your schedule.

When/then. Kent Healy, co-author, *The Success Principles for Teens,* and I have discussed this phenomenon and he coined it the *when/then* concept.

"**When** I have more time, **then** I will…

"**When** this semester/quarter is over, **then** I will…

"**When** I finish college, **then** I will…

If you've ever said something like this to yourself, you know that most of the time it's just a way for your mind to trick you into procrastinating. Your mind pushes things into the future so that you don't do anything different now.

And, since we're talking about time, the irony is that there is no future. There is only now. Even in the future, if you choose to do something different, you are choosing to do it in that moment, which is always now. So, if you're waiting for something to happen in order for you to start making time for the things that are most important to you, when might be a good time to begin? Now!

Ideal schedule. When making time for the things that are most important to you in your life, even if you're on the semester system, I'm curious what your ideal schedule would look like for the next quarter? Quarters are a great marker for things. Not only do businesses use them for planning, but quarters usually start around the beginning of each season (which is around the 22nd of September/Fall, December/Winter, March/Spring, and June/Summer). And, if you take the time to notice, people usually require different things based upon the type of season (more sleep in the winter, more exercise in the summer, etc.).

So, when looking at the upcoming quarter, when would you ideally like to go to sleep, wake up, eat, exercise, date, hang out with your significant other, attend classes, study, work, hang out with friends, etc.? Write it all down. Be specific. Once you write this down, there are two steps to actually making it happen…

1. **Ask.** Many of the things that are most important to you will involve others. And, as I've previously discussed, a major component to having healthy relationships is effective communication. Therefore, you may want to speak with certain people about your new plan. For example, you might ask your boss, "This upcoming quarter, I would ideally like to work Tuesdays, Thursdays, and Sundays from 5−9 pm, is this possible?" Many people don't get what they want because they don't ask for what they want.

   And speaking of asking, as you're looking at making time for the things that are most important to you, you might want to look at where you can ask people to do certain things for you. And, no, I'm not talking about having someone else do your homework. But I'll bet there are things you can delegate. One time at a meeting, I asked each of my five college student interns to assist me with various business tasks that opened up an entire extra day in my calendar that week!

   People might say no to your requests and so you may need to reassess your ideal schedule accordingly, but you won't know unless you ask. And, by the way, saying no to other people's requests that don't reflect what's most important to you isn't a bad idea, either.

2. **Calendar.** Once you get your ideal schedule solidified, then put it in a calendar. Yes, creative people, a calendar. If you don't have a calendar, go buy one. If you have one, use it. It doesn't have to be anything fancy. I've used a basic calendar that you write in for years.

   Once you get a calendar in front of you, I recommend scheduling out the basics of your entire quarter.

And, don't forget, you will need to schedule time in your calendar to schedule these things. ☺

Ask me! If you ever attend my *College Life Success Boot Camp* ask me what I'm doing during that quarter at any given time and I'll look in my calendar and tell you. This doesn't mean that I can't re-arrange things if necessary. As a matter of fact, I consciously re-evaluate what's most important to me every quarter. But, in the meantime, I make sure that I'm making time for the things that are most important to me at that point in my life.

You may not be able to re-arrange your entire schedule right now because you're in the midst of a semester/quarter but, if you're currently not making time for what's most important to you, I'll bet you can start to shift some things around. Then, if you to choose to do so, you can begin to plan ahead of time so that the next quarter reflects your ideal schedule!

Creative within structure. Although this may all sound very structured, here's the beauty; you can be creative *within* this structure. Let me give you an example…

If you opened up my current calendar, you'd notice that this quarter I have "self-care" scheduled on Monday, Wednesday, and Fridays from 3:30 — 5 pm, and Saturdays from 12 — 4 pm. It actually says "self-care" instead of something like "run on the treadmill." Why? Because, while specificity and routine can be useful, what usually happens after about two weeks of "running on the treadmill" to take care of yourself? If you're like most people, it gets boring. And, when things get boring, what do people usually do? Stop. If you're interested in consistently taking good care of yourself, variety works wonders. Then, depending upon what you feel like doing during that time and day, you can choose accordingly.

It's 1:35 pm right now. I'll be doing something in two hours to take care of myself. If I was tired, I may choose to take a nap. If the surf was good, I may choose to go surfing. If the sun was out, I may choose to go for a bike ride. However, I'm not tired, the surf isn't good, and it's raining. Therefore, I'm going to go to the gym. My choice may be different in two days, depending upon what I feel like doing then. That's the creative part. The structured part is that it's scheduled. Although you can schedule all aspects of your life in this way, many people have the biggest challenge scheduling time for themselves.

Value. Perhaps the biggest fear for many people in our culture is that, if they make time for themselves, they will lose valuable time; time that can be used to do more or accomplish things. Because, if you're not using your time to be productive, you might feel like you don't have value. Have you ever done absolutely nothing? I mean nothing. Are you still valuable then? We are trained in our culture that our value lies in what we do and not necessarily who we are; unless who you are is tied into what you do.

Quantity/quality. The busier you are and/or the more you accomplish, then the more valuable you must be. It's what keeps some students overwhelmingly busy during the school year, enrolled in extra classes, and intent upon graduating early. While the quantity of what you do is important, so is the quality; and, often times, because people don't make time for themselves, the quality of what they do is greatly affected. Have you ever neglected taking good care of yourself and noticed how it decreased the quality of an assignment you worked on? Have you ever noticed the opposite? Taking good care of yourself is one way to access being more present in what you do. And, when you are more present, the quality of what you are doing increases. You might want to consider that you lose both valuable time as well as your ability to experience your inherent value each moment you are unable to be present.

Turtle/hare. As the old story goes between the turtle and the hare, faster isn't always better. However, this doesn't give you an excuse to take longer to accomplish something, either. There are plenty of people who are unable to be present even at a slower pace. And, some college students will stay in school for as long as they can because they've placed so much of their value in being a student that they are scared of where they will derive their value after they graduate.

The point is, like the point in the story of the turtle and the hare, while something like graduating from college may be an important end goal, don't forget about the moments of time that exist between now and then. The only question becomes, "Can you value yourself enough to make the time to discover what's most important to you, put it in a calendar, and actually follow your schedule? Speaking of value, this leads directly into something that is literally valuable…money.

ACTIONS

1. When speaking about how you spend your time, practice using language that reflects powerful choice. For example, "I'm *choosing* to go to class, then to work," as opposed to, "I *have* to go to class, then to work."

2. Make a list of every *when/then* in your life that pertains to time. For example, "When I

have more time, then I will take better care of myself." Consider taking action now on what you're fantasizing about happening in the future.

3. Including all areas of your life, write out your "ideal schedule" for the upcoming quarter. Communicate with anyone necessary for solidification. Once the basics are solidified, schedule everything out in your calendar; including a time each week where you schedule out the specifics of your upcoming week. Practice being creative within this structure. And, if you don't have a calendar, go get one!

4. Look at all areas of your life and see where you can delegate something(s) to create more time in your schedule. Then delegate.

5. Practice saying "no" to things that aren't important to you.

6. Take 5 minutes right now and do absolutely nothing.

MONEY

"Money won't make you happy, but neither will being poor."

~Tony Robbins

Tattoos. When I was about to transfer from community college, I considered attending San Diego State University. I wanted to go there for three reasons; it was known as a party school, it was by the beach, and there were a lot of good-looking girls. So, my friends and I took a surf trip down the coast of California to check it out. Although I didn't end up going there, that trip played a significant role in me deciding to spend thousands of dollars on tattoos my last few years of college. Yes, I have tattoos on both of my arms from my shoulders to almost my elbows, and on my back. And, oddly enough, one of them is of burning money...more on that story in a minute.

Links. What did my trip to San Diego have to do with influencing my decision to get a bunch of tattoos? Well, as human beings, we make some unconscious links about things in our mind. For example, when I was in San Diego that week hanging out at the beach, I noticed that there was a common denominator among the guys who were surrounded by good-looking girls; they all had lots of tattoos. Here's the unconscious link I made…

"Guys with a lot of tattoos are surrounded by good-looking girls."

"I want to be surrounded by good-looking girls."

"Therefore, I will get a lot of tattoos."

This might sound stupid, but we make these links all of the time; even when it comes to money.

Burning money. Speaking of stupid, I mentioned that one of my tattoos is of burning money. Perhaps even more stupid is why I chose to permanently anchor that image on my body. During that time in my life, I had witnessed many events that led me to believe money was "the root of all evil." So, the link I made was something like…

"Money is the root of all evil."

"I don't want to be associated with evil."

"Therefore, I don't want anything to do with money."

Guess how much money I had as a college student? Not much!

Poor students. You don't have to think money is the root of all evil to not have much money as a college student. After all, just like self-care, it's pretty much expected from both the college culture and the culture at large that students don't. When I first started my business, you wouldn't believe how many people warned me that college students didn't have money. That one belief in and of itself could be significantly hampering your ability to have more money.

"College students don't have money."

"I am a college student."

"I'm not supposed to have money."

College students can have more money and, in addition to their beliefs, this possibility is also influenced by their willingness to promote themselves.

Self-promotion. Whether you're interested in making more money or being in a romantic relationship, you're going to have a challenging time making these things happen if you don't promote yourself. As a matter of fact, sometimes working isn't that much different from dating.

Dating. If you go to my website, **www.collegelifesuccess.com**, you'll find out that the purpose of my business is to support college students from around the world in living more successful lives. Other than this book, you'll also discover that there are three major ways in which I have supported college students in doing so…

1. **SPEAKING**
2. **BOOT CAMP**
3. **COACHING**

When I'm presenting *The 4 Secrets to College Life Success* **SPEAKING EXPERIENCE** at colleges throughout the United States, I mention the opportunity to purchase my book for those students wanting more in-depth information. And, if the college is near my home in California, I also share about *The 4 Secrets to College Life Success* **BOOT CAMP** that I put on for students interested in taking immediate action on the information in the book. Then, on the last day of my Boot Camp, I offer my group and individual **COACHING** programs for students who are interested in reaching their fullest potential. Notice all of the self-promotion? ☺

Just like someone you'd like to date, as you can see, after each event I ask students if they'd be interested in spending more time with me. It's like meeting someone at a huge party for the first time. After hanging out with them for an hour or so, you decide to ask them to join you and a bunch of your friends and go on a trip for a weekend. After sharing the weekend together, you ask them to hang out more regularly in a group; or, if you really click, you ask them to hang out with you individually. That's similar to what it's like for me, only I'm running a business.

Whether you are running your own business, interviewing for a job, or asking for a promotion within a current job, just like me and my business, one of the only ways you're going to make more money is if you promote what you have to offer.

Fear. One of my past public speaking students asked me one time what my biggest fear was when I spoke. After some contemplation, I answered, "Promoting my products and services. I'm afraid that students will think I'm just there to sell them something."

Public speaking is one of the biggest fears for many people. One major reason why people are so scared of it is because they are afraid of what people might think of them when they're up there. For example, although someone might say that they're afraid they'll forget what to say, what they're probably most afraid of is, if that happens, people will think they're stupid, etc. So, looking at the answer I gave the student about my own fear, when it really comes down to it, I'm afraid that students will think I'm egotistical. And, believe it or not, the following "link" happens to be one of the major reasons why people don't promote themselves.

"People who promote themselves are egotistical."

"I don't want to be viewed as egotistical."

"Therefore, I won't promote myself."

So, rather than promote themselves and risk being viewed a certain way, when given the opportunity, like public speaking, people will choose not to (or barely).

Humility. While not promoting yourself might be considered an act of humility, for many, it's an unconscious way that people avoid valuing themselves and what it is they have to offer. Even people who promote themselves can use self-promotion as a way to cover up the fact that they don't value themselves and what they offer. As a matter of fact, this is when people usually experience someone as egotistical. However, in my experience, promoting something that will benefit others, no matter how much you value yourself or what you have to offer, will humble you faster than anything else because, believe it or not, it's ultimately not about you.

It's not about you. Another public speaking student once asked me what my most challenging experience was for me while speaking. One time, I was speaking to the largest college student audience I had been in front of up until that time; 400 student-athletes. About three quarters of the way through the presentation, everything in me tensed up so strongly that I wanted to run off stage. This experience not only lasted for the rest of the presentation, but continued as I drove back home. In the midst of my severe physical and emotional anguish, all I could think about was never speaking again. Seriously. However, something in me said, "It's not about you."

Having taught public speaking for numerous years, I've always encouraged students to stop making so much of their speaking experience about themselves and focus on making a difference with their audience. After all, that's a large purpose of speaking. So, if I'm speaking and begin thinking to myself, "What if these students think that I'm trying to sell them something?" I mention my products and services anyway. Even though there might be students in the audience who think I'm egotistical, if I don't offer the opportunity because I'm afraid of what people might think of me, guess who loses out? Those who would benefit from what I have to offer! Who is possibly losing out on what you have to offer due to any of your own resistance to self-promotion?

Career. Don't get me wrong, promoting my products and services, although a major reason why I do what I do, isn't solely about the students' benefit. I also do what I do to make money; after all, I am running a business. I have a wife and two kids to support and, if you haven't noticed, even if you aren't married with kids, you need to make money somehow. Would I do what I do if I didn't need to make money? Absolutely. For the most part, I love what I do. Which reminds me...

Growing up, I witnessed my Dad work his way up the corporate ladder and, from my perception, each step he climbed, although he made more money, the more he seemed to dislike his job. As I was contemplating career paths in college, I remember thinking, "People who make a lot of money must hate their career. I'd rather love my career and not make much money."Ironically, guess what career I went into? Teaching! How many teachers do you know that say they love what they do? How many teachers do you know that don't make much money? Talk about a link! It was only later on in life that I realized this was just an unconscious belief and it was actually possible to love my job and make a lot of money.

Fantasy. And, if you noticed, earlier I shared with you that I love what I do...for the most part. I've come to the realization that it's a fantasy to think you're going to love what you do all of the time. Another fantasy was, part of me went into teaching because I thought, unlike the corporate world, it would be less competitive. Come to find out, it's just as competitive, if not more. So, just like any other career that provides people with money for their life, it was still necessary to promote myself in order to get hired! And, remember, it's not only about promoting what you can *do*, but who you *are*.

Be-Do-Have. Robert Kiyosaki, author of the #1 New York Times Bestseller *Rich Dad, Poor Dad*, discusses the concept "Be-Do-Have" in his book *Cashflow Quardrant*. He basically talks about how, when someone wants to "have" something, like more money, they usually focus on what they need to "do" to get it. For example, in this chapter I've encouraged you to promote yourself in order to have more money.

However, people often fail to consider who they must "be" in order to do what they need to do to get what they want to have. For example, he mentions how a person's beliefs are an important component of this (you're not going to promote yourself to have more money if you think self-promotion is egotistical). He also adds how, similar to what I discussed about communication, that who a person is *being* has a lot to do with who they show up as. For example, if you want to find the perfect romantic partner, you could go do many different things to look for the right person, but you might want to work on being the right person first and foremost.

While it may be true that who you are being will effect you getting what you want, what most people don't realize is that they usually want whatever they want because they think it will make them be a certain way. When I have more money, then I will be_____.

Covet. In his book *Instant Enlightenment,* David Deida shares the following two pieces of wisdom…

1. Act like you would feel if you had everything you wanted. Or,

2. Ignore your desires because they don't lead to happiness in any case.

Teacher. "How would I show up as a teacher if I was making one million dollars per year?" This is the question I began to contemplate at one point during my career when I noticed a strong desire to have my *College Life Success* business generate a more lucrative income and, ultimately, replace my job teaching college.

I remember one particular quarter that I really put this question into practice and, long story short, a few students of mine ended up telling their baseball coach about how much they enjoyed my class; probably because of how I was showing up more fully. Because of this, it opened up the opportunity for me to meet with their coach who eventually hired me to speak privately to their team, played a key role in me speaking to all of the student-athletes at that college, and introduced me to numerous college coaches all over the United States…all having to do with generating a more lucrative income from my *College Life Success* business.

The fact of the matter is that, even if all of those things would not have happened, I remember that quarter being one of the most deeply satisfying experiences of teaching. Although the outcome was rewarding, it was who I was *being* that was most satisfying.

Money is important. This doesn't mean that whether or not you are able to act like you would feel if you had all of the money you wanted, you should completely ignore your desire for it. Simply don't place so much emphasis on the happiness you think it will eventually bring. Money may not be the most important thing in life, but it is important. It's important for your survival as well as anything else that might support your life choices.

For example, a few years after I got all of my tattoos and realized the primary reason for getting them was due to my personal insecurities, I went to see a doctor who specialized in tattoo removal. Guess how much money it would've cost me to remove them all…burning money bags included? $28,000! Talk about irony.

And, in addition to your life, money can support other people's lives as well. What do most charities need to support other people? Money! Money is important. And so is how you manage it.

Money management. I'm sure you've heard of at least one professional athlete, celebrity, or CEO who had millions of dollars and lost it all? Yes? While there may be many reasons for why this happens, one big one is because most people don't know how to effectively manage the money they have. And you don't have to be a millionaire for this to be important. No matter how much money you currently make and/or are given by your family, contrary to popular belief, college students have money. As a college student, I had enough money to spend thousands of dollars on tattoos. You have money. Just like your time, it's simply a matter of what you choose to do with it. Unfortunately, when it comes to money management, most people only know how to do one of two things with their money; spend it or save it.

Spend or save? Creative people tend to spend their money, while structured people tend to save it. Whatever your tendency, in my opinion, the most effective money management system on the planet that is both creative and structured, was created by T. Harv Eker, author of the #1 New York Times Bestseller *Secrets of the Millionaire Mind*. While he goes into more detail about it in his book, which I would encourage you to read, I'd like to share with you the basics.

Jars. At the end of each month, after taxes, take the remaining amount of money you have, divide it into the following percentages, and put it into the respective jar accounts…yes, actual jars.

1. **50% — Necessities.** Your necessities account includes things such as rent, food, insurance, etc.; things that are <u>absolutely</u> necessary.

2. **10% — Financial Freedom.** This account is specifically designed for you to invest money in things that will enable you to not have to work in the future.

3. **10% — Play.** The idea behind this account is that, every month you blow ten percent of your income on something fun! What I love about this account is that it supports structured people in being more joyful and creative people in not blowing all of their income. ☺

4. **10% — Long-Term Savings for Spending.** This account is for things you want, but need to save up for. Things like a new car, vacation, new computer, etc.

5. **10% — Education.** Whether it's a book *like this*, a weekend seminar *like my Boot Camp*, a Life Coach *like me*, etc., this account is all about your continuing education (the *life applicable* education that isn't always taught in school).

6. **10% — Give.** Remember me mentioning how money can support other people's lives as well? This is the account. Donate to a charity, help out a family member, etc.

As you can see, although this money management system is a structure, just like a schedule, it allows for tons of creativity within it.

Now. And, just like your time, it's vitally important to begin managing your money now; even if it means starting out by using 90% of your income for your necessities. Because, despite you possibly thinking you'll manage it once you have a certain amount, you more than likely won't. Start now and watch how it can support everything you use money for; including the next topic, your living environment.

ACTIONS

1. What are 1—3 "links" you've made about money and/or self-promotion that may be contributing to you not having more money?

2. Practice self-promotion. Get present to who you are and what you have to offer and, despite any fear, begin sharing your gifts. Consider that, if you don't, in addition to you, others lose out as well.

3. Practice being who you would be once you've "made it" financially. How might you show up differently in life?

ENVIRONMENT

"Have nothing in your houses that you do not know to be useful or believe to be beautiful."

~William Morris

Field trip. If this book was part of a college course you were taking and the entire class took a field trip right now to where you currently live, what would they notice about your environment? How is your living space decorated? Is it messy or organized? And, how do such things contribute to both how you feel as well as how you perform?

Feng shui. Have you ever experienced walking into a hotel, someone's home, a teacher's office, a restaurant, etc. and noticed how it made you feel? This may have been largely due to an ancient Chinese concept called feng shui (pronounced *fung shway*). In Karen Rauch Carter's book *Move Your Stuff, Change Your Life*, one of the most practical and useful books I've ever seen on the subject, she states that, "Proper feng shui is purposefully arranging the stuff around you to gain positive results." Just like managing your time and money, your environment is already arranged a certain way; it's simply a matter of whether or not it's arranged most effectively. Whether you live in a dorm or mansion, using the principles of feng shui can support you in creatively arranging your environment in order to receive various life benefits; including feeling better.

Spring cleaning. Speaking of which, whether you use feng shui or your own creative methodology, have you ever noticed how, when you make the time to optimally arrange your environment, you feel a greater sense of energy and vitality?

Unfortunately, most people only do this about once per year and, in the United States, we call it spring cleaning. Shortly thereafter, people's environments tend to get messy again and the energy and vitality that was originally generated from their environment begins to dissipate; usually until the following spring. The challenge becomes being able to sustain an optimal environment not only for optimal energy, but optimal performance.

Performance. Have you ever noticed how it's harder to get your homework done when working in a room that's cluttered and messy versus a room that's neat and organized? So, if an organized room is an optimal environment to work in, then, after it's optimally organized, how does one sustain optimal organization?

Mini-organizations. After you get your environment optimized, do what I like to call "mini-organizations." Simply take a few minutes at the end of each day to re-organize things as opposed to a few days at the end of each year. And, even if you decide to practice this, it doesn't mean that you'll be able to sustain it all of the time.

Lesson. As a matter of fact, if you tend to be an extremely structured person, it can actually be beneficial for you to allow things to get really messy sometimes. After all, life can be chaotic and, as much as you may try, you can't control it. Performing in the midst of a mess can be a very powerful practice. On the other hand, this doesn't give you an excuse to be messy (creative people). Channeling your creativity in a structured manner can actually produce extraordinary results...just like taking your dreams and putting them into a step-by-step goal-setting strategy.

ACTIONS

1. Beginning with your room, creatively and optimally organize your environment.

2. Practice doing regular mini-organizations in order to maintain your environment.

GOAL-SETTING

"98% of people don't write down goals"

~Jack Canfield

Survey. Being as a significant portion of the professional life coaching training I received revolved around supporting people in their goals, after I became a Life Coach, I began surveying my students on the first day of class regarding whether or not they consistently set goals for themselves. Then, after I began speaking at colleges, I started surveying other students as well. Interestingly enough, my results proved to be very consistent with what Jack Canfield, co-author of the #1 Best-Selling Book Series *Chicken Soup for the Soul,* shared when he spoke at a seminar I attended; that 98% of people don't write down goals. And, from my experience, more people don't even set them.

Goal-setting. Because setting goals for yourself can give you both a sense of intentionality with regards to where you're going in life as well as require you to show up more fully along the way, one of the very first things I have my coaching clients do is to set 1—4 specific goals they would like to work on with me during the year we spend together. However, you would be surprised at, when asked to do this, how many people respond with, "I don't know."

I don't know. I've worked with thousands of people from around the world and I have one conclusion about human beings; they have immediate access to knowing. So, when someone says, "I don't know" in response to setting specific goals for themselves, it often means one of three things...

1. I need more time

2. I don't want to tell

3. I don't want to know

I need more time. Similar to what I mentioned in the *Self-Care* chapter regarding questions I've asked students about what type of coaching support they need and what truly nurtures them, sometimes people don't know what their goals are simply because they haven't taken the time to find out. People are often too busy and don't make the time to contemplate and get clear on such things. All they might need are a few days, a few hours, a few minutes, or even a few seconds.

Ever notice in class how, when a teacher asks a student to answer a question and the student doesn't know the answer right away, that the student is very rarely given more than a few seconds to figure it out? If the answer isn't spit back instantaneously, the teacher will often immediately ask another student the question, ask the student a different question, or maybe even give the student the answer. And, if the teacher doesn't give the student the answer, you can almost bet that someone in the class will shout it out. In my experience, if students are just given a few seconds to sit with the question, without the interruption from the teacher or other students, more than likely they will come up with the answer; especially if it's a question about them…unless they don't want to tell.

I don't want to tell. I love the scene in the movie *Fight Club* where, in the back alley of a convenient store, Brad Pitt puts a loaded gun to the convenient store worker's head. He asks him for his wallet and then tells him he's going to die. As the man starts hysterically crying, Brad Pitt finds his expired community college student identification and proceeds to ask him what he studied. The man answers, "Stuff."

"Stuff, were the mid-terms hard?" Brad Pitt asks sarcastically. "I asked you what you studied!" screams Pitt, as he hits him in the head with the gun.

"Biology, mostly," stutters the man in-between his desperate cries.

"Why?" yells Pitt in a strong and piercing voice.

"I don't know," cries the man.

"What did you want to be?" Pitt asks slowly and firmly. After a brief moment of silence with no answer, he cocks the gun trigger that's being held to the back of the man's head and says, "The question was…WHAT…DID…YOU…WANT…TO…BE?"

By this time, as Brad Pitt is about to shoot the guy in the head, Edward Norton Jr. (who plays Brad Pitt's conservative friend in the movie) is freaking out about witnessing the whole situation, and the convenient store worker finally blurts out, "A veterinarian!"

I don't want to know. When push came to shove, the man knew the answers to the questions; he just didn't want to tell. How come? While there may be many reasons for this, he probably didn't want to reveal what he knew for the very reason that people who, on some level, wouldn't want to even know the answers to such questions; because it would require more of them than most people are willing to experience.

"More schooling?" asks Pitt, as he un-cocks the trigger.

"Too much schooling," cries the man, seemingly stressed out by the thought of going back to school.

"Would you rather be dead, die here, on your knees, in the back of a convenient store?" asks Pitt. "I'm keeping your license," claims Pitt.

"If you're not on your way to becoming a veterinarian within six weeks, you will be dead."

Unfortunately, many people would rather die than actually move forward on what they innately know to do. And, in our culture, it's not necessarily a physical death (although it could be), but a spiritual death. Because, essentially, people's lack of action on what they innately know to do is what subtly, day by day, kills people's spirit. There's nothing wrong with being a convenient store worker if that's what you're called to do, but it wasn't the case for this guy.

Goal-acting. Although the title of this chapter is goal-setting, knowing and setting your goals are one thing, actualizing them is an entirely different ballgame. Taking powerful action in alignment with your goals, aka "goal-acting," can support you in actually doing so; and that's where an effective step-by-step plan of action can be useful.

Plan of action. Let's say that one of your goals by the end of this upcoming school year is to obtain a 3.5 overall G.P.A. Once you've written down this end goal, the next plan of action would be to write down your goals for each quarter along the way. However, before you do, because everyone is different, the end goal that you set will be more powerful if you ask your-self a few key questions…

1. Do I tend to set myself up for failure by setting unreal-istic goals?

2. Do I tend to undervalue myself by setting unusually

low goals?

3. Do I tend to set goals that are about what I would ex-
    pect to happen anyway; goals that are ordinary?

4. Is this something that would be nice or am I actually
    committed to it?

Even if you have never set a goal for yourself before and/or
written it down, by simply reflecting upon your life and how
you typically approach it, you will be able to answer the above
questions.

Stretch-goals. Whatever your answers might be, when setting
specific goals for yourself, I encourage you to set goals that will
stretch you, but not b-r-e-a-k you. So, if your consistent G.P.A.
is 2.0, a goal of 3.5 may be a great way to set yourself up for
failure right off the bat. It would be like setting a goal of bench-
pressing 300 pounds by the end of the year, when you currently
can only do 100 pounds. If you know anything about weight-
lifting, it's not going to happen. However, you also probably
wouldn't set an end goal of bench-pressing 110 pounds. Similarly, if your consistent G.P.A. is 2.0, an end goal of 2.2 might
not be enough of a stretch. Remember, goals that stretch you,
but not break you. The way you tend to approach life in general
as well as your specific situation will determine the most powerful way to set your goal. This can apply to any area of your
life that you set an end goal for, as well as your plan of action
that will support you in achieving it.

Quarterly plan. As I mentioned before, once you've powerfully
set your end goal, the first step in your plan of action would be
to write down your goals for each quarter along the way; your
quarterly plan. Given the timeline of most college students'
academic calendar, these milestone goals would probably be

around December and March; September would be your starting quarter and June would be the end goal.

Going back to our original example, let's say that you decided to keep the goal of obtaining an overall 3.5 G.P.A. because, based upon your consistent 3.0 G.P.A., it seemed like an appropriate stretch. So, in order to reach this goal, your goals at each quarter along the way would be...

September— (Start)

December— 3.3

March— 3.5

June— 3.8

If you add these 3 numbers together and divide by 3, you'll find out that the overall G.P.A. is 3.5...the end goal.

Gradual. You'll also notice that there's a gradual increase throughout each quarter. As much as you might want to hit your end goal right away, no matter how excited you might be at the beginning to do so, it often works wonders to approach it gradually. Too much pressure to achieve a long-term goal immediately will often have a detrimental effect. However, when you approach reaching an end goal gradually, it often relieves unnecessary pressure and frees up energy that, paradoxically, may support you in hitting your end goal even sooner. This doesn't mean that there won't be times when it might be more useful to stretch yourself like you never have before in a short-period of time; it's just not as effective as an on-going long-term strategy. And, speaking of on-going long-term strategies, after you've set your quarterly goals, the next step in the plan of action is to create an action plan.

Action plan. Similar to the self-care "Top 4 list," an action plan consists of the 1 – 4 most powerful actions that, if you did daily *and* weekly, would increase your chances of hitting your goal. For example, if your next quarterly goal is a 3.3 G.P.A., your action plan for the upcoming quarter might look like…

1.   Attend all classes (daily)

2.   Study for 2 hours (daily)

3.   Visit professors' office hours (once/week)

Other. There may be other powerful actions that you can't take daily or weekly that would serve to increase your chances of hitting your quarterly goal. You may want to create an "other" category and list 1 – 4 things that you could do every other week, every month, once per quarter, etc. For example…

1.   Attend a study group (once/month)

2.   Attend *College Life Success Boot Camp* (see website for dates)

Key. The key is to focus on actions that are in alignment with your next quarterly goal. This doesn't mean that it's not useful to keep your end goal in mind or regularly visualize it happening, but don't lose focus on what's right in front of you. As a matter of fact, because I'm a visual learner, it's worked really well for me to type everything out and, literally, place it directly right in front of me on my office wall; which, in this context, would look something like…

GOAL

3.5 Overall G.P.A

QUARTERLY PLAN

December – 3.3

March – 3.5

June – 3.8

ACTION PLAN (through December)

Daily and weekly:

1. Attend all classes (daily)

2. Study for 2 hours (daily)

3. Visit professors' office hours (once/week)

Other:

1. Attend a study group (once/month)

2. Attend *College Life Success Boot Camp* (see website for dates)

And, if you decide to set a few more goals for the year (I recommend no more than 4 total), you can add onto this piece of paper. When it's all complete, the final step in the plan of action is to schedule your action plan into your calendar. Remember the calendar I recommended you use? Then, all that's left to do is follow your schedule.

Re-evaluate. At the end of the quarter, based upon whether or not you follow your schedule (combined with other factors), you will have either hit your quarterly goal or not. This is a great time to re-evaluate your process along the way to your end goal. Make some time at the end of each quarter to reflect upon what worked, what didn't work, and the most powerful way to proceed forward. After re-evaluating whether or not to keep your original goals or adjust them accordingly, based upon your next quarterly goal, put in place the same or newly revised action plan.

Reward. Just like writing down goals, most people don't reward themselves. And, if they do, it's usually a random act as opposed to a purposeful reminder of their powerful efforts. Whether or not you hit your goal, I highly encourage you to reward yourself at the end of each quarter; maybe new clothes if you do, or a new CD if you don't. And it doesn't have to cost anything, either. Be creative. Either way, rewarding yourself in some way can serve as positive reinforcement for something that most people don't even do.

ACTIONS

1. Set 1−4 goals for this upcoming school year (you can also do this for shorter periods of time). Take into consideration the questions I invited you to ask yourself when setting goals (Do I tend to set myself up for failure by setting unrealistic goals? Do I tend to undervalue myself by setting unusually low goals? Do I tend to set goals that are about what I would expect to happen anyway; goals that are ordinary? Is this something that would be nice or am I actually committed to it?). Next, create a quarterly plan, followed by an action plan.

2. Post the above somewhere you can see it, put the action plan in your calendar, and follow.

3. At the end of each quarter, re-evaluate. Reflect on what's working/not working, make any necessary adjustments, and reward yourself.

SURRENDER

"You can't always get what you want, but if you try sometimes you just mind find you get what you need."

~The Rolling Stones

Surrender. Have you ever noticed that you don't always get what you want; that you're not in as much control as you think? And, how that can be a really good thing? ☺ I'm absolutely clear that if everything throughout my life would have happened in the exact way that I wanted it to, you would not be reading this book. This doesn't mean, like the stereotypical meaning of surrender implies, that you should give up and do nothing. As a matter of fact, it's quite the opposite. Consider that surrender, in this context, means to take action in the areas of self-care, relationships, time management, money, environment, and goal-setting as powerfully and authentically as possible, trusting that, no matter what, life will lead you to exactly where you need to go. And, in the context of this book, this leads you into the fourth, and final, secret...

SECRET #4

ACTION

Awareness. Have you ever read a textbook for school and noticed, at the end of each section, there were questions to answer about the material? You've probably been assigned such questions as homework, right? And, because it was homework, you probably either did it because you felt as though you had to, or you didn't do it at all. You probably noticed, similar to a textbook that, throughout this book, I've included specific actions to take related to the material? However, different from most textbooks, I hope that the material I've revealed thus far has been useful about how to thrive in your life during and after college. And, because of this, I hope that you took on some of the actions at the end of each section because you wanted to or, if you didn't, would like to at some point. Awareness is useful, but taking action on what you know would be valuable for you to do is where the rubber hits the road.

Action NOW. If you've taken <u>all</u> of the actions that I've presented at the end of each section, you can skip ahead right now to where I discuss **support**. However, if you're like most people, you probably haven't taken <u>all</u> of the actions. It's ok. And, in the spirit of action, I have some coaching for you that I'm going to invite you to take action on NOW. It entails you taking action on the following <u>four</u> things…please read the first thing, take the action, read the next thing, take the action…and so on; until all <u>four</u> things are completed.

1. Circle <u>one</u> of the following three secrets that would be most powerful for you to take action on in your life right NOW.

SELF-CARE

HEALTHY RELATIONSHIPS

CREATIVE STRUCTURE

2. Re-read <u>all</u> of the actions in that chapter. Put a check mark in the following box after you've read all of the actions. ☐

3. Pick the action that would be most powerful for you to do. Circle it in your book.

4. Take the action. Please put down your book and take the action NOW! Come back to reading the next paragraph below entitled **more coaching** when you are finished…

More coaching. You have just either followed <u>all</u>, <u>some</u>, or <u>none</u> of my coaching instructions regarding the <u>four</u> things I invited you to take action on and, depending upon what you did or didn't do, I have some more coaching for you. Please skip to the section "ahead" that is in alignment with how many of the <u>four</u> things you just took action on; <u>all</u>, <u>some</u>, or <u>none</u>. And, as tempting as it may be, it will only take away more of your valuable time to read the sections that don't apply to you. So, please follow my coaching instructions and skip down to the appropriate section.

All. Congratulations! I hope that the action you took was powerful for you and your life. My only coaching to you at this point would be to notice whether you took action on each one of the four things because you thought you should or because you innately wanted to. Whatever the case may be, I invite you to keep taking action based upon what's most powerful for YOU. Now, please skip ahead to where I discuss **support**.

Some. First of all, congratulations on taking some action! I'm curious; after you began taking action on some of the four things I invited you to, what was your BIGGEST reason for not completing the rest of the actions? (For example, you might have said to yourself something like, "It's useless, I am tired, I am anxious to move forward, etc.") Contemplate this now until you come up with your own simple answer.

Got it?

Next, write your answer down big and bold on a separate sheet of paper. So, it might look something like…

I AM TIRED

I invite you to consider that what you just wrote down on your sheet of paper is probably the biggest reason that not only stops you from taking action, but prevents you from fully showing up *in your life*. Heck, you may not have written it down just now because of this very reason. So, if you didn't write it down on a separate sheet of paper, the first piece of coaching for you is to write it down NOW.

Then, once it's been written down, go get some tape and post it somewhere in your home where you can see it every day. Begin to notice when this reason prevents you from not doing things that would be valuable for you to do; then practice taking action anyway.

To begin this practice, I invite you to go back to the four things that I originally invited you to take action on and finish what you didn't. Taking this one simple action will support you in breaking up a pattern in your life that's been preventing you from more fully showing up. Take the action NOW. *After* you have completed the rest of the actions, please skip ahead to where I discuss **support**.

None. First of all, since you didn't take any action on my previous coaching, congratulations on taking it now! You are already making progress. ☺ My sense is that, if you're like most people who hardly take action on what they know would be valuable for them to do, it would be most powerful for you to continue doing what you just did; taking one small action at a time. So, with regards to the four things I invited you to take action on that you didn't, I invite you to go back to the first of the four things and take that action NOW. This simply means flipping back a few pages and circling something. That's it. If, after doing that, you feel like you want to do more, that's your choice. I don't care either way. However, when you're finished, please then continue your reading below where I discuss **support**.

Support. When it comes to taking action, contrary to how most people have been trained in our culture, I highly encourage you to ask for and allow support. Because, no matter how much people innately know that taking a certain action would be valuable for them, often times, it's only through the support of others that they actually do it.

Me. I began writing this book almost four years ago. As soon as I began to write, I started telling people. While it may be necessary and appropriate not to share something you're doing or wanting to do, most of the time telling others can act as an initial way to enlist support. It's kind of like telling your best friend that you're going to ask someone out; they're more than likely going to eventually check-in with you. If you tell the right people, it creates instant accountability. Over the past four years, I have had countless people, through asking me how my book was going, presence me to my commitment to getting it complete.

In addition, over the years, I have directly asked numerous people for their support. As I'm writing this sentence, my book completion deadline is in four days. I have not only told eight people in my life about my deadline, but I've asked them to support me in very specific ways over the next few days. My job now is to simply allow them to support me. After all, if it weren't for my previous students and clients allowing me to support them, you wouldn't be reading this book because most of the material in it wouldn't exist. Remember, allowing support is a gift for you, but it's also a gift for the people supporting you.

Awards. Speaking of support, have you ever watched an award show or been at an award ceremony and witnessed someone walk up to receive it and seriously say into the microphone, "I have nobody to thank." I haven't. If you're like me, you've seen people being dragged off stage, heard loud music being played to cut them off, etc. because the list of people they wanted to thank for their support was longer than the show or ceremony had time for! Whether you ever receive an award or not, support from others is crucial to living a successful life.

My list. Although people are often thanked for their support on the first few pages of other people's books, I've included my list right here in the midst of it. To be honest, when reading someone else's book, because I usually don't know anyone and it's at the beginning, I usually just skip right over it. While you probably don't know anyone that I'm about to mention, in the spirit of support, I wanted you to at least see how many people (that I can remember) have come into my life to support me since the beginning of my career up until the completion of this book. With that being said, I would like to extend a heartfelt thank you to the following people…

1. Jennifer Acosta-Pardoe
2. Coral Pardoe
3. Curren Pardoe
4. Tom Pardoe
5. Gloria Pardoe
6. Elisa Pardoe
7. Tom Pardoe, Sr.
8. Carlyne Pardoe
9. Nick Infantino
10. Becky Infantino
11. Julie Guglielmelli
12. Mike Infantino
13. Cresencio Acosta
14. Judy Acosta
15. John Amaral
16. Christina Amaral
17. Genyana Amaral
18. Isabelle Amaral
19. Noelle Acosta
20. Christopher Acosta
21. Kasey Acosta
22. Cory Shelton
23. Bobby Richards
24. Randy Fujishin
25. David Denzler
26. Ashla Kinnaman
27. Greg Vlamis
28. Dennis Jaehne
29. Wen-shu Lee
30. Phillip Wander
31. Shawn Spano

32. Andy Wood
33. James Lull
34. Liz Harris
35. Beth Von Till
36. Stephanie Coopman
37. Mia Hoglund-Kettman
38. Kim Pearce
39. Alex Kramer
40. Elaine Lee
41. Rob Schweitzer
42. Mary Immig
43. James Redfield
44. Donald Epstein
45. Parker Palmer
46. Tony Robbins
47. David Deida
48. Ken Wilber
49. Adyashanti
50. T. Harv Eker
51. Robert Kiyosaki
52. Suze Orman
53. Gary Zukov
54. Phil McGraw
55. Drew Pinsky
56. Oprah Winfrey
57. Eckhart Tolle
58. Thomas Kinkade
59. Jack Canfield
60. Karen Rausch Carter
61. Charles Muir
62. Gary Chapman
63. Deepak Chopra
64. His Holiness The Dalai Lama
65. Roy Eugene Davis

66. Marianne Williamson
67. Carolyn Myss
68. Wayne Dyer
69. Stephen Covey
70. Ellen Grace O'Brian
71. Sundari Jensen
72. Suzanne Samson
73. David Sunday
74. Sylvia Karuna Lunt
75. Perry Spencer
76. Damon Mahoney
77. Tammy Pittenger
78. CJ Nelson
79. Michael Scott
80. Estee Horn
81. Sonja Stewart
82. Eric Andelman
83. Hans Phillips
84. Desiree Phillips
85. Christopher McAuliffe
86. Cathy Morrey
87. Paul Anselmo
88. Sherry Anselmo
89. Cindy Bacon
90. Bret Ranoa
91. Bert Parlee
92. Terry Patten
93. Jordan Luftig
94. Alexis Loevenich
95. Jacques Bickett-Belet
96. Tristen Kunze
97. Jodi Lamont
98. Shawn Carroll
99. Brett Dugan

100. Kiersten Dugan
101. Gali Kronenberg
102. Bill Hastings
103. Jay Salamon
104. John Curotto
105. Joe Crowley
106. Mervin Ison
107. Jonathan Martinez
108. Stan Karp
109. Jon Robertson
110. Alicia Robertson
111. Jan Hutchins
112. Tanja Lippert
113. Ryan Lippert
114. The Hotel Los Gatos
115. Patti Rice
116. Jeff Morrison
117. Betty Montoya
118. Frank McCue
119. Marianne Bickett
120. Yvonne Falk
121. Anna Meck
122. Jane Artz
123. The Pruneyard Plaza Hotel
124. Kent Healy
125. Christopher Otazo
126. Skip Getz
127. Bonnie Getz
128. Alan Wagner
129. Lenna Wagner
130. Carol Knight
131. Betty Ensminger
132. Darrell Batchelder
133. Darlene Batchelder

134. Sharla Jacobs
135. Jesse Koren
136. Kay Harrison
137. Patti Yukawa
138. Jennifer Wagner
139. Lenore Harris
140. Brenda Anholtz
141. Meg Laxier
142. John Hannigan
143. Paul Sanders
144. Susan Hoisington
145. Matt Long
146. Brady Fuerst
147. Mark O'Brien
148. Staci Gustafson
149. Jason Stock
150. Dan Coonan
151. Rusty Weekes
152. Steve Kalush
153. Sunwolf
154. Paul Soukup
155. Craig Gower
156. Diane Guerrazzi
157. Katie Heintz
158. Fern Siliva
159. Helen Otero
160. Chris Changras
161. Bruce Watson
162. Jesse Wilkins
163. Cristan Cannon
164. Larry Resneck-Sannes
165. Daniel Blumberg
166. Lee Holden
167. Rachel Abrahams

168. Jonathan Tallman
169. Barry Vissell
170. Karen Elliott
171. Sydney Altano
172. Tiffany Fullmer
173. Hope Teasdale
174. Michelle Poen
175. Mistie Lonardo
176. Amaya Swanson
177. Justin McSharry
178. Joelle Collins
179. Bernadine Rosso
180. Shen Cunningham
181. Debbie Barber
182. Gerald Bittner, Jr.
183. Miriam Diaz
184. Ali Niemiec
185. Jason Burdick
186. Tom Lonardo
187. Lindsay Hammons
188. Kaitlin Dahill
189. Deanna Schlemmer
190. Cassandra Camilleri
191. Andrea Carrera
192. Anjuli Christ
193. Irene Truong
194. Jacquelyn Starke
195. Nayeli Montano
196. Lauren Adamson
197. John Montgomery
198. Pamela Velazquez
199. Lauren Mitcheom
200. Kelsey Houlihan
201. Tyler Moran

202. Veronica Garcia
203. Maxine Goynes
204. Meaghan Jones
205. Tina Kim
206. Evan Sarina
207. David Mauntz
208. Alex Varnava
209. Garrett Logan
210. Scott Freeman
211. Darrin Nelson
212. Beth Goode
213. Candice Piper
214. Ralph Frey
215. Aivar
216. Michael Engh
217. Jim Briggs
218. Jim Purcell
219. Anne Mota
220. Ingrid Williams
221. Paul Fitzgerald
222. Olivia Kei
223. Jerry Smith
224. Jerrold Shapiro
225. Linda Reilly
226. Sue Pidhorney
227. Eric Saperston
228. James Malinchak
229. Devon Mohammed
230. Darshan Shanti
231. Roberta Ross
232. Paul Salamone
233. Robb Smith
234. Alison Shellman
235. Amy Shellman Smet

236. Susan Money
237. Lily Hills
238. Karen Hudson
239. Jeanne Rosenberger
240. Martine Sweeney
241. Marika Riggs
242. Gary Riggs
243. Frank Andrews
244. Buford Barr
245. Rosemary O'neill
246. Amanda Dohse
247. Kenrick Ali
248. Kevin O'Connor
249. Jerilyn Chuman
250. Liz Cipres
251. Bob Kopecky
252. Dan McGinty
253. Rob Mieso
254. Howard Irvin
255. Michelle Donohue
256. Pauline Le
257. Paul Boese
258. Tod Burnett
259. Mindy Zemrak
260. Simon Senzon
261. Monica Parikh
262. Bill McGovern
263. Stephanie Motzkus
264. Don Dodson
265. DeAnna Batdorff
266. Mike Clark
267. Kate Schulte
268. Michael Robinson
269. John Muller

270. Russ Leal
271. Marie Rector
272. KQED
273. Joya Winwood
274. Rhonda Harper
275. Monique Lombardelli
276. Kristin Schuerlein
277. Michael Gavin
278. Rich German
279. Monica Pizzuti
280. Emily Bauer
281. Jim Donovan
282. Bob Merrick
283. Courtney Macavinta
284. Greg Reid
285. Arielle Ford
286. Rhonda Farber
287. Terry Peluso
288. Sari Smith
289. Connie Coutain
290. Mike Robbins
291. Kim Woodland
292. Nancy Samsel
293. Sally Donnelly
294. George Durando
295. Brian Fisher
296. Steve Spitalny
297. Julia Capocelli
298. Brendon Burchard
299. Mike Koenigs
300.

You. In addition to the thousands of other unnamed people who have, in some way, contributed to this book coming to fruition, I would like to personally thank you. Yes, you. You'll notice that I left person #300 blank. That space is for you. Even though I don't know you, I've had you in mind the whole time I've been writing. ☺ Thank you for providing the futuristic support I needed to take action on completing this book.

ACTIONS

1. Make a list of everyone in your life that supports you.

2. Practice asking for and allowing support. Thank people when they do.

3. Consider taking <u>every</u> action at the end of each section until <u>all</u> of the actions are completed. Schedule them in your calendar. Get an accountability partner to support you.

   OR

   Go to **www.collegelifesuccess.com,** click on BOOT CAMP, and register. It's a weekend designed to support you in taking action on everything in this book within <u>two</u> days!

Boot Camp

Lecture	5%
Reading	10%
Audio-Visual	20%
Practice by Doing	75%

According to the different ways listed above in which people learn most effectively, you hopefully received twice as much out of reading this book than if you attended a SPEAKING EXPERIENCE. And, if you are interested in receiving over 7 times more value from the information in this book, I highly encourage you to register for the next BOOT CAMP. This action alone just might be the most powerful action you take from this entire book!

To register, simply go to **www.collegelifesuccess.com**.

* Also, if you live outside of the Bay Area and are unable to attend the event in person, an audio-visual version of the BOOT CAMP is available via the website.

REFERENCES

INTRODUCTION

Fujishin, Randy. *Gifts from the Heart*. Lanham, MD: Rowan & Littlefield, 2003.

Team-in-Training. www.teamintraining.org

SECRET #1: SELF-CARE

Wilber, Ken. Patten, Terry. Leonard, Adam, and Marco Morelli. *Integral Life Practice*. Boston, MA: Integral Books, 2008.

Accomplishment Coaching. www.accomplishmentcoaching. com

Donald Epstein. www.donaldepstein.com

SECRET #2: HEALTHY RELATIONSHIPS

Mitch Hedberg. www.mitchhedberg.net

Bateson, Gregory. *Mind and Nature: A necessary unity*. Hampton Press, 2002.

Redfield, James. *Celestine Prophecy*. New York: Warner, 1993.

Ellen Grace O'Brian. www.csecenter.org

Chapman, Gary. *The Five Love Languages*. Chicago, IL: Northfield, 2007.

Tolle, Eckhart. *The Power of Now*. Novato, CA: New World Library, 1999.

Hans Phillips. www.ontoco.com

Chopra, Deepak. *The Path to Love.* New York: Harmony, 1996.

SECRET #3: CREATIVE STRUCTURE

Healy, Kent, and Jack Canfield. *The Success Principles for Teens.* Deefield Beach, FL: HCI, 2008.

Tony Robbins. www.tonyrobbins.com

Kiyosaki, Robert. *Cash Flow Quadrant.* New York: Warner, 1999.

Deida, David. *Instant Enlightenment.* Boulder, CO: Sounds True,2007.

Eker, T. Harv. *Secrets of the Millionaire Mind.* New York:HarperCollins, 2005.

Carter-Rauch, Karen. *Move Your Stuff, Change Your Life.* New York:Fireside, 2000.

Canfield, Jack, and Marc Victor Hansen. *Chicken Soup for the Soul.* Deerfield Beach, FL: HCI, 2001.

Fight Club. 20th Century Fox, 1999.

NOTES

LaVergne, TN USA
13 January 2011
212239LV00003B/1/P